feel good,
look great!

# feel good, look great!

p

# contents

# →introduction

→ This book concentrates on the latest research, yet the theory that natural foods have therapeutic benefits is hardly new. In the distant past there was probably little distinction between food and medicine. Today, scientific research into the effects of certain foods on health has supported long-held beliefs that eating the right foods in the right balance can have a positive impact on our health.

→ The foods that are believed to offer specific health benefits have become known as 'healing' foods. However, it is important to understand that just because, for example, apples are good for us, it is not beneficial to eat them in excessive quantities. Healing foods should become part of a daily diet that is intrinsically balanced, and which also gives us pleasure.

→ In the chapters that follow, you will find up-to-date information and recipes demonstrating how we can all improve our health and well-being. Getting a balance of nutrients is fundamental, and selecting the best ingredients and preparing them in particular ways will ensure you get the most from your food. In the Looking and Feeling Great sections, we identify which foods make us look and feel good, tackling areas such as skin, hair and nails, and diseases like heart disease and cancer. The A–Z of Nutritional Healing covers conditions from acne to PMS, explaining how they can be relieved through diet. Finally, the practical Healing Foods Directory enables you to select those foods that will work best for you personally, helping you achieve good health, vitality and peace of mind.

Fruits and vegetables are nutrient-dense foods, which means they have a high amount of vitamins and minerals in comparison to the calories they contain. They are generally low in fat, rich in antioxidants and protect us from the most prevalent diseases.

*Try to eat at least 5 portions of fruit and vegetables a day – a mix of different types and colours is preferable.*

**B**alance and variety are the key to planning an optimum diet. This means eating a good range of carbohydrate and protein foods, plenty of fruit and vegetables and moderate amounts of fat to ensure you get the nutrients vital for good health.

# optimum diet

### FRUIT & VEGETABLES

Aim for a minimum of 5 portions a day. A portion equals one medium-sized apple; a banana; 2 plums; a handful of tomatoes; a large bowlful of salad; a 100 g slice of melon or 90 g cooked green vegetables.

Fruit and vegetables are referred to by nutritionists as 'nutrient-dense' foods. This means that they have a high amount of vitamins and minerals in comparison to the calories they contain. They are generally low in fat, rich in antioxidants, known to protect us from the most prevalent diseases, and a good source of fibre. Organic produce – which is grown without the use of chemical fertilizers and pesticides – is becoming increasingly popular and available at supermarkets, farmers' markets and greengrocers.

Try to eat a variety of fresh produce in a range of colours, from red and yellow peppers, oranges, carrots and berries to green leafy vegetables such as broccoli, cabbage, cauliflower and chard to provide your body with a powerful combination of phytochemicals (see below) and the antioxidants beta carotene and vitamin C.

When cooking vegetables, steaming or stir-frying will retain more nutrients than boiling. Try to eat raw vegetables or salad at least once a day. Freshly squeezed juices have more nutrients than concentrated or long-life alternatives; a 100 ml glass will account for one of your 5 daily portions. Frozen fruit and vegetables can be just as high in vitamins as fresh, perhaps more so, if the fresh alternative has been stored for some time. Canned produce contains fewer nutrients, and you should opt for no sugar or salt varieties whenever possible.

### PHYTOCHEMICALS

RECENT RESEARCH HAS IDENTIFIED A NUMBER OF NATURAL PLANT COMPOUNDS THAT COULD PLAY A CRUCIAL ROLE IN PREVENTING HEART DISEASE, ARTHRITIS, DIABETES AND CANCER. THESE COMPOUNDS ARE KNOWN COLLECTIVELY AS PHYTOCHEMICALS AND MAY, IN THE FUTURE, BE CLASSIFIED AS ESSENTIAL NUTRIENTS. FRUITS AND VEGETABLES, WHOLEGRAINS, NUTS, SEEDS AND PULSES CONTAIN A RANGE OF PHYTOCHEMICALS.

*healing foods*

Around 50 per cent of our daily diet should be made up of carbohydrate foods and they should form a part of every meal, since they supply the body with the sustained energy that it needs to function effectively.

## WHOLEGRAINS, CEREALS AND POTATOES

*All carbohydrate foods provide sustained energy. Unrefined varieties are richer in nutrients and fibre.*

Aim for 6–11 servings a day. A portion is a slice of bread, a bowl of cereal, 1 medium potato or ½ cup cooked cereal, rice or pasta.

This group includes cereals, bread, rice, noodles, pasta and potatoes, otherwise known as carbohydrate or starchy foods. Some 50 per cent of our daily diet should be made up of carbohydrate foods. They should form a part of every meal, since they supply the body with the sustained energy that it needs to function effectively.

The more unrefined the better. Foods containing refined and processed grains and cereals not only contain fewer nutrients but lead to yo-yoing blood sugar levels, the effects of which are mood swings and variation in energy levels. Wholemeal is better than white, because these foods provide more fibre, B-group vitamins and minerals (see Vitamin and Mineral table on pages 20–23). Fibre helps to protect against digestive disorders and heart disease and comes in two forms: insoluble fibre helps to prevent constipation and bowel disorders by speeding up the passage of food through the large intestine. Whole wheat, brown rice and nuts are good sources of insoluble fibre. Soluble fibre, found mainly in beans, vegetables and oats, can reduce harmful blood cholesterol and help control blood sugar levels.

Carbohydrate foods are often accused of being fattening but it tends to be what you serve with them, such as butter, cheese or creamy sauces, that bumps up the calories and fat levels.

*Protein is vital for growth and repair. Eat moderate amounts daily to ensure you get a complete range of essential amino acids.*

## MEAT, FISH AND PROTEIN ALTERNATIVES

Aim for 2–3 servings a day. A serving equals 115–175 g lean red meat, 115–140 g white fish; 2 eggs; 5 tbsp beans or 2 tbsp nuts.

Moderate amounts of lean meat, poultry, fish, Quorn, eggs, pulses, nuts, seeds and tofu are recommended on a daily basis, but try to eat a variety to ensure a good balance of amino acids. This group of foods is essential for growth, repair and maintenance in the body, and provides valuable amounts of iron, B-group vitamins, zinc, magnesium, vitamin E and fibre.

The body requires protein in relatively small amounts, so foods from this group should make up around only 10–12 per cent of the daily diet. Limit red meat to 3 servings a week and try to eat oily fish, such as sardines, tuna, salmon, herring and mackerel, twice a

week. These fish contain rich amounts of omega-3 fatty acids, which are thought to reduce the risk of heart disease. Limit your egg intake to 4 a week.

Since animal sources of protein can be high in fat, it is important to balance this with plant forms found in beans, peas and lentils. These are low in fat and high in fibre. Nuts and seeds are nutritious, are a good source of the essential fatty acid omega-6 but are relatively high in fat, so eat on a regular basis but in moderate amounts.

The high-protein diets that are currently fashionable may not be good for you in the long term. Studies have found a link between a high protein diet and constipation, bowel disease and an increased risk of osteoporosis, since in excess protein encourages the excretion of calcium from the bones. Additionally, too much protein in the long term may affect kidney function.

Eat a good range of carbohydrate and protein foods,

plenty of fruit and vegetables and moderate amounts of

fat to ensure you get the nutrients vital for good health.

*Low-fat dairy foods
and fats are the
healthiest option.*

recommended that children under the age of two should not be given low-fat dairy produce such as semi-skimmed milk. Children over two years can be given semi-skimmed milk but not skimmed, providing they are eating a varied, balanced diet.

Organic dairy produce is preferable as it is free from antibiotic residues, growth hormones and agrochemicals. Soya, oat or rice milk make good alternatives to cow's milk and are also a good source of calcium.

## MILK & DAIRY FOODS

Aim for 2 servings a day. A serving equals a 300 ml glass of milk; 25 g Cheddar cheese; 1 small pot of yogurt.

Milk, cheese, yogurt and fromage frais provide valuable amounts of protein, calcium, some B-group vitamins, including $B_{12}$, $B_6$ and $B_2$, as well as vitamins A and D, essential for healthy teeth and bones and the release of energy from food. Nutritionists advise that this group of foods should make up about 15 per cent of our daily diet.

Dairy produce, particularly hard cheese, can be high in saturated fat, so opt for low-fat varieties. Children, however, need a certain amount of fat, and it is

## FATS

Aim to eat sparingly.

A certain amount of fat is necessary for good health – in fact, too little has been linked to depression – but it is essential to eat the right type. Fat is mainly used by the body as energy, providing and transporting vitamins A, D, E and K around the body. The Department of Health recommends that fats should make up no more than 35 per cent of total calories, although many nutritionists believe the figure should be 30 per cent.

There are two main types of fat: saturated and unsaturated. There is a proven link between too much saturated fat and high cholesterol, plus an increased risk of heart disease, cancer and obesity. It is important to minimize intake of animal fats in particular, including meat, cheese, cream and butter, and opt for lean and

*Choose natural live bio yogurt
to help maintain a healthy
intestinal environment.*

*healing foods*

low-fat versions. Saturated fat is also found in milk chocolate, biscuits and cakes. Margarine, once hailed as the healthy alternative to butter, is often laden with additives, preservatives and hydrogenated or trans fats, which have been found to be even worse for your health than saturated fat. When buying margarine look for those that are non-hydrogenated. This type of fat is also often found in processed foods.

Unsaturated fats, both polyunsaturated and monounsaturated, can help to reduce harmful 'LDL' (Low Density Lipoprotein) cholesterol – the type that furs up the arteries. Polyunsaturated fats provide the essential fatty acids, omega-3 and omega-6. Oily fish, walnuts, soya beans and rapeseed provide omega-3, while omega-6 is found in vegetable oils, nuts and seeds. Essential fatty acids have been found to reduce the risk of heart disease, cancer, skin complaints, arthritis and PMS. Monounsaturated fat, found in olive oil, rapeseed oil, olives and avocados, not only reduces harmful LDL cholesterol in the body but maintains or raises good 'HDL' (High Density Lipoprotein) cholesterol levels. There is also a link between monounsaturated fat and a reduced risk of heart disease and cancer, along with increased life expectancy.

*Oily fish contain essential fatty acids, which reduce your risk of heart disease and cancer.*

*Try to drink 6–8 glasses (1.7–2 litres/ 3–3.5 pints) of water a day.*

## WATER

Water plays a vital role in maintaining good health but few of us drink enough. It delivers nutrients around the body, regulates body temperature and transports waste. It is best to choose filtered or natural mineral water to achieve the desired daily amount. Coffee, tea and fizzy drinks contain caffeine, which has a diuretic effect, so they actually dehydrate the body. Herbal or rooibosch (red) tea are healthy, caffeine-free alternatives.

*optimum diet*

The way you shop, store and prepare your food can affect its nutritional status. The following tips will help you get the most from your food.

## SHOPPING TIPS

⊙ Whenever possible buy organic, seasonal and local produce. You may have to pay slightly more, but the foods are usually fresher, more nutritious and less damaging to the environment than foods flown thousands of miles and kept in cold storage for months.

# optimize your foods

⊙ Buying from a farmers' market or direct from a farm is a good way to source fresh produce – it can also be cheaper.

*For optimum freshness, buy little and often.*

⊙ Buy fresh foods from shops with a high turnover of goods. Avoid fruits and vegetables that are displayed on the roadside or in a hot, light window, since nutrients will be diminished. Fluorescent lighting also depletes nutrients.

⊙ Buy fresh produce in small quantities on a regular basis and remove them from plastic bags when storing. Loose fresh produce is also much easier to check for quality.

⊙ When shopping, purchase or choose chilled and frozen foods last to keep them cool, avoid spoilage and possible growth of bacteria.

⊙ When buying fresh meat, fish and shellfish, it is easier to check quality and freshness if buying over the counter. Wild or organic salmon and trout are preferable to farmed fish. Undyed smoked haddock and cod is better than the highly coloured, bright yellow alternatives.

⊙ Check labels when buying packaged foods. Avoid those with high amounts of sugar, saturated and hydrogenated (trans) fat, colours, additives, flavouring, preservatives and artificial sweeteners.

⊙ When buying eggs, look for organic, free-range. Farm-fresh or boxes depicting attractive countryside scenes mean nothing: the eggs are usually from battery farms. Organic eggs come from hens that have been better looked after, and are not routinely fed antibiotics or yolk-enhancing dyes.

*Whenever possible, buy local produce in season.*

⊘ The terms 'natural', 'country' or 'traditional' mean little when used on processed foods.

⊘ You pay for what you get – if buying processed foods, opt for good quality such as sausages and burgers with a high meat content and minimum amount of fat and fillers. Choose fish without batter or breadcrumbs, which can be an excuse for manufacturers to add colours, preservatives, fat and cheap fillers.

⊘ Look for farm assurance schemes, which approve production standards and quality of ingredients, when buying meat and poultry.

## STORING & COOKING TIPS

⊘ Depending on the type of fruit or vegetable, store in a cool larder or in the bottom of the fridge. Avoid keeping them for too long, since nutrients diminish with age. Some fruits such as bananas, melons, peaches and avocados can be ripened at room temperature.

⊘ Raw fruit and vegetables are generally the most nutritious. Avoid peeling them, if possible, since many nutrients are found in or just below the skin.

⊘ Do not prepare fruits and vegetables too far in advance of cooking or serving as nutrients diminish as soon as cut surfaces are exposed to the air.

⊘ Steaming is preferable to boiling – the latter destroys water-soluble vitamins such as C and B-complex. Stir-frying is another good way of retaining nutrients. If you boil vegetables, use as little water as possible and do not overcook them. The cooking water can also be kept and used to make stock for soup or sauces.

⊘ Buy nuts and seeds in small quantities and store in an airtight container in a cool, dark cupboard. Don't keep them for too long as they can become rancid. Herbs, spices, pulses, flour and grains should be kept in the same way.

⊘ Store oils in a cool, dark place to prevent oxidation.

*optimize your foods*

15

Deciding which foods to cut back on is just as crucial as what you choose to include in your diet. Foods high in sugar, fat and salt provide the body with negligible nutrients and can do more harm than good.

## SUGAR

Refined sugars and those found in processed foods, including biscuits, sweets and cakes, have little or no nutritional value. Eating a sugary food gives a temporary surge in energy, which is promptly followed by a slump.

# what to avoid

It is this fluctuation in blood sugar levels that leads to an inconsistent supply of energy to the brain, leading to poor concentration, mood swings, brain 'fug' and tiredness. Many sweet foods combine sugar with fat, so tooth decay and weight gain are both consequences of eating too much of these foods.

Moderation is the key. Don't deny yourself completely, but try to restrict eating sweet foods to after a meal to avoid swings in blood sugar. When shopping, look out for sucrose, fructose, glucose, maltose, corn syrup, invert sugar and dextrose on food labels, which are basically sugar by another name. Honey and maple syrup are marginally better as they contain a few minerals, but they have the same effect on blood sugar levels.

*Recent studies show that sugar has an ageing effect on the skin – not to mention the detrimental effect on teeth and weight.*

*A bowl of cornflakes contains more salt than a packet of crisps.*

Many low-sugar foods contain artificial sweeteners, such as saccharin or aspartame, which have been linked to hyperactivity in children as well as diarrhoea if eaten in excess. They also perpetuate a sweet tooth.

## SALT

On average the British eat 12 g of salt a day – 4 g is the upper recommended amount – most of which is found in processed foods. Crisps, crackers, salted nuts, stock cubes, packet soups and cheese are obvious culprits but, surprisingly, a bowl of cornflakes is higher in salt than a bag of crisps. Other processed foods that contain high amounts of salt include biscuits, baked beans and bread. The salt we need is supplied in adequate amounts in natural foods such as meat, fish and vegetables. Excess salt is a major cause of high blood pressure, which leads to strokes and heart attacks. Too much salt in the diet has also been linked to fluid retention and kidney stones.

## CAFFEINE

Caffeine is a stimulant, which means it helps to keep us alert and awake. If drunk in excess (over 8 cups a day), however, it can lead to the jitters, shakes, headaches, an irregular heartbeat and stomach upsets. It is also a diuretic, causing dehydration in the body. Those at risk of osteoporosis should pay special attention to their caffeine intake, since it increases the excretion of

*Herb teas are naturally caffeine-free.*

calcium in the urine. It also inhibits the absorption of vitamins and minerals from the gut.

Coffee contains about 40 per cent more caffeine than tea and chocolate. Strong continental brands, in particular, are more likely to have noticeable side effects. Fizzy drinks, like cola, also contain caffeine. Try to limit yourself to no more than three caffeine drinks a day. Herbal teas and coffee alternatives are healthier options.

17

Moderation is the key. Try to restrict eating sweet foods

to after a meal, reduce your salt and caffeine intake and

limit your alcohol intake to 14 units a week for women

and 21 units a week for men.

Heavy drinking can lead to depression, insomnia, anxiety and forgetfulness. It can also increase the risk of osteoporosis, certain cancers, heart disease, impotence and brain and liver damage in the long term. Alcohol is an appetite suppressant, so those who drink too much risk being deficient in nutrients. Additionally, alcohol affects the absorption of vitamins A, B, C and D, essential fatty acids, calcium, zinc, magnesium and phosphorus.

*If drunk in excess, alcohol affects the absorption of nutrients from food.*

## ALCOHOL

The latest research shows that not all alcohol is bad for you. Red wine, for example, has been found to help prevent heart attacks. Antioxidants known as flavonols are the key, since they help to make the blood less prone to clotting. Antioxidants also help to mop up harmful free radicals in the body by reducing cell damage, known to cause cancer. Whisky is also said to raise antioxidant levels.

Moderation, however, is vital. Although drinking around two units of wine or beer a day may reduce the risk of heart disease, women should not exceed 14 units of alcohol a week, men 21 units. Avoid binge drinking and spread your intake throughout the week, keeping two consecutive days completely alcohol-free.

*The long-term effects of pesticide use are unknown.*

## ADDITIVES

The most commonly used additives are colours, preservatives, flavour enhancers, emulsifiers, flavourings and glazing agents. Not all additives are potentially harmful, but some have been linked to hyperactivity in children, poor memory, depression and mood swings.

Although additives have to be listed on food labels, they are not always easy to spot. Since the backlash against 'E numbers', some manufacturers have taken to describing them by their generic name. The flavour enhancer monosodium glutamate (E621), for example, is routinely added to flavoured crisps. MSG has been linked to a range of symptoms known as 'Chinese restaurant syndrome', including dizziness, anxiety, mood swings, pain in the chest, palpitations, sweating, headaches and asthma attacks. Avoiding additives altogether is difficult. The simplest option is to reduce the amount of processed foods you buy, opting for fresh, unadulterated foods instead.

## PESTICIDES

Despite government reassurances that pesticides used in agriculture do not exceed legal limits, we do not know enough about the long-term effects of ingesting small doses of pesticides, nor the possible danger to the body of eating these different pesticides in combination.

Common pesticides include organophosphates, herbicides, fungicides, nitrates and growth regulators. Buying organic is one way to avoid them. You can also reduce your chances of residue intake by buying good-quality, fresh produce that does not look old, wilted or mouldy. Wash all fruit and vegetables thoroughly, including pre-washed salads, before cooking or serving raw. Remove the outer leaves of vegetables or top, tail and peel them. Scrub the skin of hard fruits such as melon before cutting. By following these guidelines, you should remove half to three-quarters of whatever residue remains on your fruits and vegetables.

*Wash all fruit and vegetables thoroughly before use.*

Fruits and vegetables are obvious sources of nutrients, but a diet incorporating all food types is essential to gain a good balance of vitamins and minerals.

# essential vitamins & minerals

*A varied and balanced diet is the key to good health.*

| **⊙ BEST SOURCES** | **⊕ ROLE IN HEALTH** | **⊗ DEFICIENCY** |
|---|---|---|
| ⊙ Animal sources: milk, butter, cheese, egg yolk, margarine and liver. Plant sources: carrots, apricots, squash, red peppers, broccoli, green leafy vegetables, mango and sweet potatoes | ⊕ Necessary for vision, bone growth, skin and tissue repair. Beta carotene acts as an antioxidant and protects the immune system | ⊗ Poor night vision, dry skin and lower resistance to infection, especially respiratory disorders |
| ⊙ Wholegrain cereals, brewer's yeast, potatoes, yeast extract, nuts, pulses and Quorn | ⊕ Essential for energy production, the nervous system, muscles and the heart; promotes growth and boosts mental well-being | ⊗ Depression, irritability, nervous disorders, loss of memory. Common among alcoholics |
| ⊙ Cheese, eggs, milk, yogurt, milk, fortified breakfast cereals, yeast extract, almonds and pumpkin seeds | ⊕ Vital for energy production, tissue repair and maintenance, and the functioning of vitamin $B_6$ and niacin | ⊗ Lack of energy, dry cracked lips, numbness and itchy eyes |
| ⊙ Pulses, potatoes, fortified breakfast cereals, wheatgerm, peanuts, cheese, eggs, mushrooms, green leafy vegetables, figs, prunes, poultry, tuna and pork | ⊕ Essential for a healthy digestive system, skin and circulation. Also needed to release energy from food | ⊗ Deficiency is unusual but is characterized by lack of energy, depression and scaly skin |
| ⊙ Eggs, wheatgerm, wholemeal bread, breakfast cereals, nuts, bananas, poultry, salmon, turbot and lentils | ⊕ Assimilates protein and fat to make red blood cells; maintains a healthy immune system | ⊗ Anaemia, dermatitis and depression |
| ⊙ Milk, eggs, fortified breakfast cereals, cheese, yeast extract, liver, mussels, oily fish and lean beef | ⊕ Required in the formation of red blood cells, maintaining a healthy nervous system, and energy production | ⊗ Fatigue, increased risk of infection, anaemia |
| ⊙ Green leafy vegetables, fortified breakfast cereals, bread, nuts, pulses, bananas, yeast extract and asparagus | ⊕ Vital for cell division (growth). An increased intake is recommended pre-conception and during the first three months of pregnancy to protect the foetus against neural tube defects | ⊗ Anaemia and appetite loss. Linked to neural defects in babies |
| ⊙ Citrus fruit, melons, strawberries, tomatoes, broccoli, potatoes, peppers and green vegetables | ⊕ Helps the body absorb iron, and maintains healthy skin, teeth and bones. An antioxidant that strengthens the immune system and helps fight infection | ⊗ Increased susceptibility to infection, fatigue, poor sleep and depression |

*essential vitamins & minerals*

*Keeping active is as important as a good diet for maintaining health.*

Many nutrients in fruits and vegetables are found

in or just below the skin so prepare them carefully

to maximize nutrition.

*Fresh, unprocessed foods provide a range of beneficial, therapeutic nutrients.*

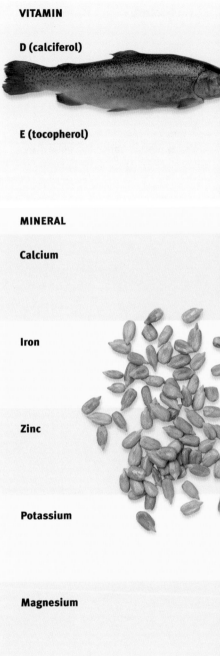

**VITAMIN**

**D (calciferol)**

**E (tocopherol)**

**MINERAL**

**Calcium**

**Iron**

**Zinc**

**Potassium**

**Magnesium**

**Phosphorus**

**Selenium**

● Margarine, vegetable oils, eggs, cereals, butter, cod liver oil and oily fish. Also sunlight

● Seeds, wheatgerm, nuts, vegetable oils, eggs, wholemeal bread, green leafy vegetables, oats, sunflower oil, avocado and fortified breakfast cereals

⊕ Helps the body to absorb calcium and phosphorus, which is vital for bone and teeth formation

⊕ An antioxidant that is essential for healthy skin, circulation and maintaining cells

⊗ Softening of the bones and muscle weakness. Long-term shortage results in rickets

⊗ Increased risk of heart attack, stroke and some cancers

● Milk, cheese, yogurt, green leafy vegetables, sesame seeds, broccoli, dried figs, pulses, almonds, spinach, watercress, sardines and tofu

● Egg yolk, fortified breakfast cereals, green leafy vegetables, dried apricots, prunes, pulses, wholegrains, tofu, seeds, lean beef, liver and brown rice

● Peanuts, cheese, wholegrains, sunflower and pumpkin seeds, pulses, milk, hard cheese, yogurt, wheatgerm, liver, Quorn, crab, lamb and beef

● Bananas, milk, pulses, nuts, seeds, wholegrains, potatoes, fruits and vegetables

● Nuts, seeds, wholegrains, pulses, tofu, dried figs, dried apricots and green vegetables

● Milk, cheese, yogurt, eggs, nuts, seeds, pulses, wholegrains, meat and fish

● Avocado, lentils, milk, cheese, butter, brazil nuts, seaweed, tuna, white fish, sardines, salmon and pork

⊕ Builds and maintains bones and teeth; maintains muscle function and the nervous system

⊕ Carries oxygen from the lungs to all the cells in the body

⊕ Essential for a healthy immune system, tissue formation, normal growth, wound healing and reproduction

⊕ Regulates body fluids, maintains normal blood pressure and nerve transmission

⊕ Keeps muscles, bones and teeth healthy. Required for normal growth and nerve formation

⊕ Essential for healthy bones and teeth, energy production and the assimilation of nutrients, particularly calcium

⊕ An antioxidant that protects against cancer, heart disease and premature ageing

⊗ Soft and brittle bones, osteoporosis, fractures and muscle weakness

⊗ Anaemia, fatigue and low resistance to infection

⊗ Impaired growth and development, slow wound healing and loss of taste and smell

⊗ Weakness, thirst, fatigue, mental confusion and raised blood pressure

⊗ Lethargy, weak bones and muscles, depression and irritability

⊗ Deficiency is rare

⊗ Reduced antioxidant protection

*essential vitamins & minerals*

# →looking great

*A healthy outer self is an excellent indication of inner health, and knowing that you look great is a wonderful confidence booster. This chapter looks at the foods that can improve the condition of skin, hair, teeth and nails, alongside useful recipes and advice on complementary remedies.*

The skin is one of the major organs responsible for eliminating toxic waste. The single most important nutrient, vital for hydrating the skin and flushing out toxins, is water.

# skin

**W**e all want a glowing, healthy, blemish-free complexion. When your skin looks good, you feel good – an excellent reason to give it a boost through a well-balanced diet.

Stress, environmental pollution, sun and lack of sleep all take their toll on our skin and, of course, genetic make-up plays a part. Poor digestion, food intolerances and allergies can also cause or exacerbate skin disorders, such as acne, eczema and psoriasis. But eating the right foods and drinking plenty of water can improve and revitalize the skin, helping to relieve existing skin problems and curbing the onset of others. The skin is one of the major organs responsible for eliminating waste. A diet high in junk foods, laced with alcohol and cigarettes, means that it has to work harder to get rid of toxic waste products and can be overloaded with harmful toxins.

The single most important nutrient for a glowing complexion is water. We should drink about 6–8 glasses a day to hydrate the skin and help flush out toxins. Other essential nutrients include vitamin A, which combats dryness and keeps skin soft; B-group vitamins to promote a glowing complexion and aid the renewal of skin cells; vitamin C to strengthen blood vessels and maintain collagen and elastin levels; vitamin E to transport nutrients to the skin cells and reduce damage by harmful free radicals; zinc to improve skin tone, encourage healing and prevent skin infections; and essential fatty acids, which contain high levels of the skin-tightening chemical dimethylaminoethanol (DMAE), so helping to maintain collagen and elastin levels, hydrate, firm and boost skin tone.

## SKIN TIPS

✚ SPEND 5 MINUTES A DAY BRUSHING YOUR BODY IN LONG, SWEEPING MOTIONS, ALWAYS TOWARDS THE HEART. SKIN BRUSHING IMPROVES LYMPHATIC DRAINAGE AND SLUGGISH CIRCULATION, SHIFTING STUBBORN CELLULITE.

## USEFUL FOODS

- ✔ Carrots, broccoli, spinach, sweet potatoes, pumpkin and apricots are all rich in beta carotene, which counters dry, flaky skin.
- ✔ Apples, artichokes, beetroot and asparagus cleanse the liver and kidneys, helping to detoxify the skin.
- ✔ Avocados provide vitamins A, C and E and valuable monounsaturated fat, which helps to keep the skin supple.
- ✔ Essential fatty acids found in oily fish and linseeds (omega-3), as well as nuts and seeds (omega-6), soften and hydrate the skin and protect against sun damage.

## AVOID

- ✖ Alcohol dehydrates the skin, creates harmful free radicals and depletes the skin of certain vitamins, particularly B-group and C. Additionally, it weakens blood capillaries, leading to thread veins.
- ✖ Smoking depletes vitamin C, causing the blood vessels to constrict and slowing down circulation.
- ✖ Processed foods provide few nutrients and are often loaded with chemical additives, colours and preservatives.
- ✖ Saturated and hydrogenated fats slow down the lymphatic system, essential for the transport of nutrients, and generate high levels of destructive free radicals.
- ✖ Refined sugar, believed to be as harmful as smoking, affects skin elasticity, leading to wrinkles and skin ageing.

## guacamole with roasted vegetables

This creamy dip is an excellent source of the antioxidants, vitamins C and E, and avocado has the highest protein content of any fruit.

**Serves 2**

**Ingredients**

1 avocado, stone removed

1 small garlic clove, crushed

1 tbsp fresh lemon juice

*Roasted vegetables*

Choose from a selection of butternut
squash, red pepper, asparagus, red
onion, courgettes, carrots and fennel,
cut into chunks

1 tbsp olive oil

few sprigs fresh rosemary

**❶**

Preheat the oven to 200°C/400°F/Gas Mark 6. Place your chosen selection of vegetables in a roasting dish. Toss the vegetables in the olive oil using your hands. Place the sprigs of rosemary on top and roast in the oven for 30–40 minutes until the vegetables are tender and golden.

**❷**

Meanwhile, make the guacamole. Scoop out the avocado flesh using a spoon. Mash with the garlic and lemon juice until fairly smooth and creamy.

**❸**

To serve, remove the rosemary sprigs and arrange the roasted vegetables on a plate. Top with a spoonful of guacamole. Serve with wholemeal pitta bread.

27

Overexposure to hair dyes and perming lotions sometimes causes hair and scalp problems, but a healthy, balanced diet will help to rectify the damage and boost condition.

# hair

**D**ull, lacklustre hair may be an indication that you are lacking in nutrients. There is a correlation between the state of your hair and your inner health and general well-being. Illness, stress or an emotional problem can all have a detrimental effect on your hair condition, which even a good haircut and the latest styling products won't be able to remedy. Overexposure to hair dyes and perming lotions sometimes causes hair and scalp problems, but a healthy, balanced diet will help to rectify the damage and boost condition.

The B-group vitamins as well as vitamins C and E, beta carotene, iron, zinc and selenium help to feed the hair and are of prime importance. Drinking plenty of mineral or filtered water – about 6–8 glasses a day – can also improve the condition of your hair. Stress can have a damaging effect on hair condition, causing scalp disorders such as dandruff. Since people suffering from stress are likely to be short of B-group vitamins, it is particularly important to include sufficient amounts of wholegrains, lean meat, poultry, eggs, nuts and pulses in the diet. Zinc is said to alleviate dandruff, and is found in shellfish, dairy products, wholegrain bread and cereals.

Significant hair loss has been linked to low iron levels. If you need to boost your intake of this mineral, increase your intake of vitamin C at the same time as this will help your body absorb the iron. Biotin deficiency can also contribute to hair loss. Although this nutrient is mainly produced by bacteria in the gut, it is also found in cooked eggs, peanut butter, liver and wholegrains.

## USEFUL FOODS

- ✔ In Japan, a diet rich in seaweed is believed to give you lustrous hair, probably on account of its high mineral content.
- ✔ Essential fatty acids found in oily fish, vegetable oils, nuts and seeds can help prevent a dry, flaky scalp.
- ✔ Lean red meat, eggs, pulses, dried apricots and green leafy vegetables are a good source of iron, which helps counter hair loss.
- ✔ Protein is vital for hair growth, making it shiny and keeping it in good condition. Opt for lean meat, chicken, fish, eggs, low-fat dairy products, pulses, nuts and seeds.

## AVOID

- ✘ Caffeine, found in coffee, tea and some fizzy drinks, dehydrates the body and inhibits the absorption of certain nutrients, including iron.
- ✘ Smoking reduces vitamin C levels in the body, which is vital for healthy hair.
- ✘ Refined carbohydrates such as white bread, pasta and rice are robbed of many of their beneficial nutrients during processing. Choose unrefined wholemeal bread and pasta and brown rice instead.
- ✘ Alternative practitioners recommend cutting down on sugar to prevent oily hair.

*Keep your locks shiny and glossy by including protein foods in your diet.*

## RECIPE

### japanese salad

This salad contains arame, a mild-tasting seaweed, which is rich in the minerals necessary for glossy hair. You can buy it at the larger supermarkets, oriental stores, or health food shops.

**Serves 2**

**Ingredients**

15 g /¹/₂ oz arame

115 g/4 oz radishes, thinly sliced into rounds

¹/₂ small cucumber, cut into thin sticks

50 g/2 oz beansprouts, rinsed

sesame seeds, for sprinkling

*Dressing*

1 tbsp sunflower oil

1 tsp toasted sesame oil

2 tsp white wine vinegar

¹/₂ tsp soy sauce

**❶**

Rinse the arame in a sieve under cold running water. Place in a bowl and cover with more cold water. Leave to soak for 5 minutes – the arame should double in volume. Drain and place in a saucepan.

**❷**

Cover the arame with cold water and bring to the boil. Reduce the heat and simmer for 20 minutes until tender, then drain.

**❸**

Meanwhile, mix all the ingredients for the dressing together in a bowl.

**❹**

Combine the arame with the radishes, cucumber and beansprouts. Spoon over the dressing and sprinkle with sesame seeds before serving.

### HAIR TIPS

➕ Brewer's yeast, which you can buy at any health food shop, is recommended for people with hair problems. It is an excellent source of B-group vitamins, iron, zinc and other minerals.

It is important to instil good habits early to ensure healthy teeth throughout life. Good care and maintenance of baby teeth helps to ensure the development of healthy adult teeth.

# teeth

A healthy diet is just as important as regular brushing and good dental hygiene when it comes to having white, clean, strong teeth.

While general dental health is better than it was in the past, we can all improve the condition of our teeth through brushing and flossing every day and eating certain foods. It is important to instil good habits early to ensure healthy teeth throughout life. Although the first set of baby teeth or 'milk teeth' are temporary, a range of nutrients and dental care are still necessary to build and maintain them. Their health also affects the development of adult teeth.

Healthy teeth require the same nutrients as strong bones, namely calcium, magnesium and vitamin D. Looking after your gums is also essential. Foods rich in B-group vitamins, beta carotene, vitamin C, zinc and folic acid will all help keep them healthy. Mouth ulcers are a sign that the immune system is compromised and that the body may be lacking in essential nutrients.

Sugar is the biggest enemy of teeth, and it is the frequency that it is eaten that increases the likelihood of tooth decay. Sugar is not only present in cakes, sweets, biscuits and fizzy drinks, but is found in many forms and in many types of food, including savoury ones. Check labels for the following: fructose, sucrose, dextrose, glucose, syrup, maltose and concentrated fruit juice. Choose savoury foods as snacks, such as vegetables, bread and cheese. Fruit is also good for teeth. However, since it contains natural sugars and is acidic, you should rinse your mouth with water after eating. Foods that require chewing help to keep teeth and gums healthy.

*Calcium is as essential for healthy teeth as it is for strong bones.*

## USEFUL FOODS

- ✔ Dairy products including cheese, milk, yogurt and fromage frais are an excellent source of calcium.
- ✔ Apricots, nuts (especially almonds), seeds, tofu, sardines, prawns, broccoli and dark-green leafy vegetables are valuable non-dairy sources of calcium.
- ✔ Magnesium, important for strong bones and teeth, is found in wholegrains, dried fruit, nuts, seeds, pulses and green leafy vegetables.

## AVOID

- ✖ Sugar in all its various forms is the number one cause of tooth decay.
- ✖ Honey is as damaging to your teeth as sugar, although it does have some therapeutic properties.
- ✖ Fizzy drinks, fruit juices, cordials and some fruit and herbal teas contain sugar. A glass of fruit juice contains beneficial vitamins, but dilute it with water to reduce its sugar content.
- ✖ Dairy and wheat have been known to trigger food allergies and intolerances, leading to bad breath. Consult your doctor before eliminating these foods.

## RECIPE

### raspberry and oat crunch

This pudding looks stunning but is very simple to make. It also makes a nutritious breakfast, providing useful amounts of calcium, and vitamins B and C.

**Serves 2**

**Ingredients**

40 g/1½ oz whole porridge oats

1 tbsp sunflower seeds

115 g/4 oz fresh or frozen raspberries
   (defrost before using)

250 g/9 oz thick natural bio yogurt

1 tbsp honey or maple syrup

**❶**

Place the porridge oats and sunflower seeds in a large, heavy-based frying pan and roast over a medium heat for 1–2 minutes until lightly toasted. Leave to cool.

**❷**

Place the yogurt in a large bowl and stir in the honey or maple syrup. Add the raspberries and fold in gently.

**❸**

Stir in the oats and sunflower seeds, leaving a few to sprinkle on top. Spoon the mixture into 2 glasses and top with the oats and seeds before serving.

Nails are made of a protein called keratin and should be strong, smooth and pink. Pale, brittle or ridged nails are usually a sign of vitamin and/or mineral deficiency.

# nails

The health of your skin and hair is reflected in the condition of your nails. Since all benefit from a well-balanced diet, it is important to ensure you eat a range of different foods.

Nails are made of a protein called keratin and should be strong, smooth and pink. Pale, brittle or ridged nails may be a sign of iron or zinc deficiency. If you suspect you are anaemic, ask your doctor for a blood test, and boost your intake of iron-rich foods. Eat plenty of vitamin C-rich foods at the same time to help your body absorb the iron. Lack of selenium, found in fish, shellfish, offal, grains and cereals, can also lead to ridged nails. White spots on the nails may be an indication of zinc deficiency, although they can also be the result of a knock.

A low-protein diet will adversely affect the condition of your nails. Not only does protein provide essential amino acids, it also encourages the absorption of iron. Meat, poultry, seafood, eggs, dairy products, nuts and pulses contain a good range of essential amino acids. Try to eat a variety in your diet, but opt for low-fat versions where possible. A deficiency of biotin, a nutrient mainly produced by bacteria in the intestine, will also affect your nails. Biotin is found in cooked eggs, wholegrains, peanut butter and liver. A shortage of B-group vitamins may lead to ridged nails. To counter this, eat wholegrains, dairy foods, pulses, seafood, meat, nuts, seeds, green vegetables and yeast extract.

*Citrus fruits, such as oranges, provide vitamin C which aids the absorption of iron, vital for strong nails.*

## USEFUL FOODS

- Citrus fruits, green leafy vegetables, blackcurrants, sweet peppers, tomatoes and potatoes provide useful amounts of vitamin C, which helps the body absorb iron.
- Oysters and other shellfish, seeds, pulses, lean meat and dairy foods are rich in zinc, which helps prevent brittle nails.
- Iron is found in offal, red meat, oily fish, mussels, dried apricots, green leafy vegetables, pulses and tofu.

## AVOID

- Tea contains tannin, which inhibits the absorption of iron. Brittle, pale nails may indicate iron deficiency.
- Heavy drinking dehydrates the body, depletes it of vital vitamins and minerals, and impairs its ability to absorb protein.
- Smoking affects the body's ability to metabolize vitamin C, essential for strong nails, and also inhibits the transport of oxygen and other nutrients throughout the body.

*healing foods*

## RECIPE

### spicy mussels

Zinc, iron and vitamin C are found in beneficial amounts in this aromatic shellfish dish. Serve with plenty of crusty bread.

**Serves 2**

**Ingredients**

1 tbsp olive oil

1 onion, finely chopped

2 garlic cloves, crushed

200 ml/7 fl oz dry white wine

4 tbsp canned chopped tomatoes

1 tbsp chopped flat-leaved parsley

¼ tsp chilli flakes

1 kg/2 lb 4oz mussels, scrubbed, cleaned and rinsed

squeeze of fresh lemon juice

black pepper

**①**

Heat the oil in a large, deep saucepan. Add the onion and cook for 8 minutes over a medium heat until softened. Add the garlic. Cook for a further 1 minute, stirring frequently.

**②**

Increase the heat, add the wine and boil for 2 minutes until reduced. Reduce the heat to medium and add the tomatoes, parsley and chilli. Simmer for 5 minutes or until reduced by a third.

**③**

Toss in the mussels, cover the pan, and cook for 5 minutes or until the mussels have opened. Shake the pan occasionally. Discard any mussels that remain closed.

**④**

Add a squeeze of lemon juice and season with black pepper. Spoon into large bowls and serve immediately.

# →feeling great

*Eating the right foods can reduce your risk of cancer and heart disease as well as improve your memory and increase energy levels. This chapter looks at the foods we should include in our diet and those that are best avoided. There are more recipes to try plus further advice on complementary remedies.*

Most experts agree that dietary changes can lessen your risk of heart disease. As little as one serving of oily fish a week may decrease your chance of a fatal heart attack by as much as 40 per cent.

**H**eart disease is a major cause of death in the Western world. While there are many risk factors, evidence suggests that diet can play an important role in protecting against this condition.

There has been a great deal of controversy over the relationship between diet and coronary heart disease (CHD). Ageing and hereditary predisposition are risk factors that cannot be altered, but high blood

# healthy heart

cholesterol and blood pressure, lack of exercise, obesity, smoking and diabetes mellitus are all controllable.

Most health experts agree that dietary and lifestyle changes can help. Certain foods have been found to reduce the risk of CHD, while others increase the risk. Recent studies have shown that as little as one serving of oily fish a week may decrease the risk of fatal CHD by as much as 40 per cent. These fatty acids thin the blood, helping to prevent blood clots and reduce cholesterol levels. Soya offers similar benefits. Folic acid, found in pulses and green vegetables, helps to reduce levels of the amino acid homocysteine, high levels of which have been linked to CHD and strokes. Fruits and vegetables – wonder-foods – provide fibre as well as generous amounts of phytochemicals (see page 8), antioxidants, vitamins C and E and beta carotene. They support the body's defence system and prevent the furring up of arteries that in time leads to heart disease.

*Garlic helps reduce blood pressure and cholesterol levels.*

## USEFUL FOODS

- ✔ Oily fish, including tuna, salmon, mackerel, sardines, herrings, may reduce the risk of CHD.
- ✔ Garlic supports the cardiovascular system and may reduce cholesterol levels and blood pressure.
- ✔ Oats, nuts, wholegrains and pulses provide insoluble fibre, which can reduce blood cholesterol. Oats can also reduce high blood pressure.
- ✔ Red wine (in moderation; consult your doctor first), apples, tea and onions contain quercetin, which has been found to reduce the risk of heart disease and strokes.
- ✔ Seeds, walnuts, wheatgerm and almonds provide omega-6 fatty acids, which lower blood cholesterol.

## AVOID

- ✘ Fatty and fried foods, particularly saturated and hydrogenated (trans) fats found in margarine and processed foods, encourage the deposit of fatty plaque in the arteries, leading to high blood cholesterol.
- ✘ Excess salt increases blood pressure, one of the causes of CHD and strokes.
- ✘ Refined sugar not only leads to weight gain if eaten in excess but has been found to raise cholesterol levels and blood pressure.
- ✘ Alcohol in excessive quantities is damaging to the heart. You should also avoid smoking and reduce your caffeine intake.

## mediterranean sardines

Providing beneficial omega-3 essential
fatty acids, sardines are excellent fuel
for the heart and are much underrated.
Serve with bread, grilled tomatoes and
a green salad.

**Serves 2**

**Ingredients**

**4–6 fresh sardines, depending on size,
    heads removed, gutted and cleaned**
**3 tbsp olive oil**
**zest and juice of ½ lemon**
**1 garlic clove, crushed**
**1 tbsp fresh oregano, chopped**
**1 tbsp fresh chives, snipped**
**sea salt and pepper**

**❶**

Mix together the olive oil, lemon zest,
garlic, oregano and chives in a shallow
dish large enough to accommodate
the sardines.

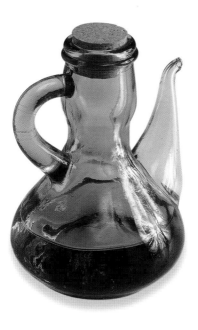

**❷**
Arrange the sardines in the dish and
turn them in the marinade. Leave
overnight in the refrigerator.

**❸**
Preheat the grill to medium. Season the
sardines with salt and pepper, and grill
for about 10 minutes, turning them
halfway through. The exact cooking time
will depend on the size of the sardines:
wait until they are golden and crispy on
the outside. Squeeze the lemon juice
over the fish before serving.

*feeling great*

Fresh produce provides protective antioxidants and phytochemicals that fight harmful free radicals and stimulate the body's defences against a range of cancers.

The World Cancer Research Fund recently reported that a staggering 40 per cent of cancers could be prevented by healthy diet and lifestyle.

Numerous studies support the argument that eating the right foods can reduce the risk of cancer, and may also play a role in supporting conventional medical treatment for the disease. Similarly, eating the wrong foods can increase the risk of cancer.

# protecting against cancer

Cancers strongly linked with diet are those of the stomach, bowel, breast, cervix, pancreas, liver and mouth. High intake of both soluble and insoluble fibre (see page 10) safeguards against the development of colon cancer and possibly that of the breast. Wholegrains, pulses, brown rice and vegetables are good sources of insoluble fibre. Along with beneficial amounts of vitamins C, E and beta carotene, fresh produce provides a catalogue of protective antioxidants and phytochemicals that fight harmful free radicals and stimulate the body's defences against a range of cancers, including lung, oesophagus and stomach. The antioxidant selenium, found in wholegrain cereals, eggs, seafood and seeds, has also been found to play a preventative role, especially against breast cancer.

A diet high in saturated and hydrogenated or trans fats may increase the risk of cancer of the bowel, pancreas, breast and prostate. Opt instead for unsaturated fats such as olive oil and those rich in omega-3 and omega-6 fatty acids found in oily fish, linseeds, nuts and seeds.

## USEFUL FOODS

✔ The powerful antioxidant lycopene, mainly found in tomatoes as well as watermelon and pink grapefruit, reduces the risk of some cancers, particularly that of the prostate. It may also safeguard against cancer of the breast, colon, stomach and lung.

✔ Soya beans, tofu, soya milk and miso contain isoflavones, believed to reduce the risk of hormone-related cancers such as those of the breast and prostate.

✔ Green tea (and black tea to a lesser degree) may protect against cancer of the colon, pancreas, urinary tract and rectum.

*Tomatoes are an excellent source of the powerful antioxidant lycopene.*

## AVOID

✘ Red meat in large quantities may increase your risk of colon cancer. Limit eating red meat to 2–3 times a week.

✘ Salt-cured, pickled, smoked, chargrilled or barbecued meats and fish have been linked to certain cancers. Eat only occasionally.

✘ Cut down on saturated fat, found in many animal protein foods and fried foods. Opt instead for low-fat alternatives.

✘ Excessive alcohol intake is recognized as a cancer-risk, as is smoking.

✘ Rancid and overheated oils and fats increase the risk of cancer. Don't store oils for a long time and avoid reusing them.

## super stir-fry

Fast and fresh, this stir-fry contains plentiful amounts of cancer-protective vegetables and seeds.

**Serves 2**

### Ingredients

½ tbsp groundnut or vegetable oil

splash of toasted sesame oil

150 g/5 oz broccoli florets

1 spring onion, sliced

75 g/3 oz pak choi, sliced

75 g/3 oz fine green beans, trimmed

1 garlic clove, chopped

1-cm/½-in piece of fresh ginger, peeled and finely chopped

1 tbsp fresh apple juice

1 tbsp soy sauce

1 tbsp sesame seeds

Heat a frying pan or wok and add the groundnut and sesame oils. Add the broccoli, onion, pak choi and green beans. Stir-fry, tossing the vegetables continuously, for 6 minutes.

**2**

Add the garlic and ginger and stir-fry for another 1 minute. Pour in the apple juice and soy sauce and cook for 1–2 minutes (add a little water if the stir-fry appears too dry) until the vegetables are just tender.

**3**

Sprinkle the sesame seeds on top and serve.

If you feel run down include plenty of B-group vitamins and iron-rich foods in your diet and – if you suspect it's a cold – minimize dairy foods.

Numerous studies confirm the link between poor diet and an impaired immune system. Weakened immunity depletes the body, leaving it more vulnerable to illness and disease.

A diet based on plenty of fruits and vegetables (at least 5 portions a day), wholegrains, lean meat, poultry, fish, dairy foods, shellfish, nuts and pulses provides a good balance of immune-boosting nutrients that will

# boost your immune system

help the body fight infections and stay healthy. Equally important are regular exercise, plenty of sleep and a positive attitude to life.

The antioxidant vitamin C, found in beneficial amounts in fruits and vegetables, packs a powerful punch when defending the body against colds, flu and infections. It also encourages the brain to produce endorphins or 'happy hormones' that lift the spirits. Other effective antioxidants – which help to protect against illness by neutralizing harmful substances or free radicals in the body – are beta carotene, zinc, vitamin E, iron and selenium.

If you feel run down include plenty of B-group vitamins and iron-rich foods in your diet such as wholegrains, lean red meat, eggs, pulses, yeast extract, dried apricots and green leafy vegetables. Quercetin, found in apples and onions, also helps to fight viruses and stop them replicating, while horseradish and watercress are good for opening up congested passages. If you catch a cold, drink plenty of fluids to prevent dehydration and eat light meals based on soups and juices to help the body purify and restore itself.

*healing foods*

40

## USEFUL FOODS

- ✔ Eat vitamin C-rich foods such as citrus fruits, berries, strawberries, broccoli, sweet potatoes, carrots and dark green leafy vegetables.
- ✔ Shiitake mushrooms are renowned in the Far East for improving immunity to illness.
- ✔ Garlic has been shown to enhance the immune system thanks to its antiviral and antibacterial properties.
- ✔ Zinc-rich foods such as seafood, poultry, lean meat, wholegrains and pumpkin seeds are vital to the production of antibodies that maintain the immune system.

*Treat yourself to some strawberries to up your intake of vitamin C.*

## AVOID

- ✘ Dairy foods should be reduced at the first sign of a cold. They are mucous forming, encouraging congestion and blocked sinuses.
- ✘ Drinks containing caffeine inhibit the absorption of valuable nutrients.
- ✘ Antibiotics are no use if you have a common cold – they cannot cure viral infections, and can compromise the health of the gut.
- ✘ Processed foods lack the nutrients necessary for a healthy immune system.

## RECIPE

### immunity-boosting juice

Help the body fight infections with this powerful combo of fruit and vegetables.

**Serves 2**

**Ingredients**

2 large carrots

2 large cooked beetroot, halved

2 apples, quartered and cored

2 oranges, peeled and quartered

150 g/5 oz seedless white grapes

4-cm/1½-in piece fresh ginger

**❶**

Juice the carrots, beetroot, apples, oranges, grapes and ginger. Drink immediately. Alternatively, process in a blender, strain, and dilute with fresh orange juice if necessary.

### IMMUNE SYSTEM TIPS

✚ THE HERB ECHINACEA IS RENOWNED AS AN EXCELLENT IMMUNE SYSTEM-BOOSTER, CUTTING THE DURATION OF THE COMMON COLD AS WELL AS ALLEVIATING ITS SYMPTOMS.

The efficient digestion of food is dependent on water: try to drink 6–8 glasses of mineral or filtered water every day.

**A** healthy digestive system is vital for general well-being. If your system isn't working efficiently, vitamins, minerals, essential fats, proteins and carbohydrates cannot be absorbed by the body.

To break down food effectively we need a balance of 'friendly' bacteria in the gut as well as digestive enzymes. If these bacteria are out of kilter due to poor diet, stress, antibiotics, illness, food intolerances or toxin

# healthy digestion

overload, conditions such as nausea, flatulence, indigestion and constipation can occur.

Certain foods can help to keep the digestive system running smoothly. Live bio yogurt contains 'friendly' bacteria that help digestion, the condition of the gut and increase resistance to infection, especially following a course of antibiotics. Sufficient intake of fibre reduces the risk of constipation, haemorrhoids and diverticulitis, an inflammation of the bowel. A diet rich in fruits, vegetables, pulses and wholegrains will ensure you have an adequate fibre intake. Bran, however, can exacerbate some digestive disorders, since it is not fully digested in the small intestine. Water is vital for the efficient digestion of food, as well as rehydrating the body following illness and preventing constipation. Try to drink 6–8 glasses of mineral or filtered water every day.

If you have recurring digestive problems, a food allergy or intolerance may be the cause. Coeliac disease, for example, is an intolerance to gluten found in wheat and cereals. Consult your doctor or a dietician if you are concerned, particularly before eliminating foods from your diet.

## USEFUL FOODS

- ✔ Live natural bio yogurt improves the condition of the gut and alleviates gastro-intestinal disorders.
- ✔ Apples are said to help cleanse the digestive system.
- ✔ Peppermint, ginger and camomile tea have a soothing effect on the digestive system and replace lost fluids following diarrhoea and vomiting.
- ✔ Certain foods, such as asparagus, artichokes, garlic, onions, bananas, tomatoes, wheat and barley contain a type of fibre that stimulates the growth of beneficial bacteria in the gut.

## AVOID

- ✘ Refined carbohydrates, including white bread, pasta and rice, contain less fibre and nutrients than unrefined, wholegrain varieties.
- ✘ Fatty foods stimulate acid production in the gut, leading to indigestion.
- ✘ Alcohol increases stomach acidity and can aggravate irritable bowel syndrome.
- ✘ Wheat bran can aggravate stomach disorders and inhibit absorption of certain nutrients.
- ✘ Curries and other spicy foods can irritate the gut.

*Apples have a detoxifying effect on the digestive system.*

## banana and strawberry smoothie

Bananas can help to prevent indigestion and ulcers, while live bio yogurt boosts and restores the condition of the gut by introducing beneficial bacteria.

**Serves 2**

### Ingredients

**2 ripe bananas, quartered**

**250 g/9 oz strawberries, hulled and halved if large**

**500 g/1 ¼ lb live bio natural yogurt**

Place the bananas, strawberries and yogurt in a blender or food processor. Process until smooth and creamy – dilute with a little milk if too thick. Drink straight away.

### DIGESTION TIPS

⊕ GO TO PAGE 64 FOR FURTHER ADVICE ON DEALING WITH CONSTIPATION AND IRRITABLE BOWEL SYNDROME, AND PAGE 70 FOR HELP WITH INDIGESTION AND HEARTBURN.

Long-term feelings of anxiety can raise both blood pressure and cholesterol levels, and increase your risk of certain illnesses.

Food has a direct effect on mood. It can induce a feeling of calm or, conversely, make you feel anxious and tense – it's important to get the balance right.

We all suffer from stress at some time or another; it is our ability to cope that varies. Perhaps surprisingly, diet can affect our ability to handle stressful situations, limiting their negative effects on the mind and body.

# achieving calm

Not all stress is bad for us, but long-term feelings of anxiety can be damaging, raising blood pressure and cholesterol levels and increasing the risk of certain illnesses and conditions, including irritable bowel, headaches and palpitations.

The frequency of meals can make a noticeable difference to tension levels. Eating regularly with the occasional healthy snack in between main meals will keep blood sugar levels on an even keel, helping you to avoid mood swings and allowing the body to cope with physical and mental pressures.

Unrefined carbohydrate foods have a calming effect on the brain. They help to transport tryptophan, the amino acid that produces the brain chemical serotonin, a natural uplifter and calmer. The B-group vitamins play a crucial role in how well you cope with stressful situations. They enable the nervous system to function well and help to release energy from the cells, which are under pressure during times of stress. Vitamin C has also been found to reduce levels of stress hormones in the blood. These vitamins cannot be stored in the body for long so need to be replenished on a daily basis. The minerals magnesium, zinc and calcium are needed in greater amounts during times of stress and a shortage will affect your ability to cope under pressure.

## USEFUL FOODS

- ✔ Omega-3 essential fatty acids are thought to have a calming effect during times of pressure. Try to include salmon, herrings, mackerel, pilchards, sardines or tuna in your diet twice a week.

- ✔ Instead of reaching for a chocolate bar, eat some fresh fruit – its natural sugars are released more slowly in the body, providing steady supplies of energy. Fruit also contains immunity-boosting vitamins, essential during stressful periods.

- ✔ Replenish stores of B-group vitamins by including wholegrains, yeast extract, dairy produce, lentils and other pulses, green vegetables, seafood, lean meat, eggs and nuts in your diet.

- ✔ Foods rich in calcium, particularly dairy products, tofu, seeds and dark-green leafy vegetables, help to reduce tension.

## AVOID

- ✘ Stimulants like alcohol and cigarettes rob the body of valuable nutrients, including vitamins A, B and C, zinc, magnesium and essential fatty acids. Alcohol is also a chemical depressant.

- ✘ Fatty and sugary foods provide few nutrients and also suppress the appetite. Refined sugar in particular leads to yo-yoing energy levels, resulting in more stress and lethargy.

- ✘ Caffeine, found in tea, coffee and fizzy drinks, inhibits the uptake of iron, calcium and magnesium. Fruit or herbal teas are a healthy alternative.

# fresh tuna niçoise

This twist on the classic French salad provides valuable omega-3 fatty acids, antioxidants and B-group vitamins, which help to counter stress.

**Serves 2**

**Ingredients**

1 tbsp olive oil

1 tbsp fresh lemon juice

2 x 150 g/5 oz tuna steaks

250 g/9 oz new potatoes, halved
   and cooked

75 g/3 oz fine green beans, cooked

115 g/4 oz mixed salad leaves

6 cherry tomatoes, halved

1 small red onion, sliced

handful black olives, stoned

salt and pepper

*Dressing*

1 tbsp extra virgin olive oil

½ tsp white wine vinegar

1 small garlic clove, crushed

3 tsp reduced-fat mayonnaise

Mix together the oil and lemon juice and season well. Place the tuna in a shallow dish and pour over the marinade. Chill for 30 minutes, turning the tuna occasionally.

Put the new potatoes, green beans, salad leaves, tomatoes, red onion and olives in a serving bowl.

**3**

Whisk together the ingredients for the dressing, then pour it over the salad and toss well using your hands.

**4**

Heat a griddle or frying pan until hot. Place the tuna steaks in the pan, brush with the marinade and cook for 3–5 minutes, turning once, until cooked on the outside and pink in the centre. Brush with the marinade when needed.

**5**

Arrange the salad on serving plates and top each one with a tuna steak.

## STRESS TIPS

✚ HERBAL REMEDIES CAN BE A BENEFICIAL ALTERNATIVE TO PRESCRIBED TRANQUILLIZERS. GINSENG HELPS TO COMBAT PHYSICAL AND MENTAL STRESS AND STRENGTHENS THE IMMUNE SYSTEM. ECHINACEA IS A WELL-KNOWN IMMUNE SYSTEM-BOOSTER, WHICH IS DEPLETED DURING TIMES OF STRESS. GOLDEN SEAL IS ALSO HELPFUL.

*feeling great*

Eat small but regular meals to sustain energy levels and keep your blood sugar levels steady.

**M**any factors can zap your energy reserves, including illness, lack of sleep and bad diet. You can improve your energy levels by reviewing what you eat.

Depleted energy can have a detrimental effect, both physically and mentally. One of the best energizers is sleep, which is something most of us lack in varying degrees. Diet is another factor – when feeling stressed and

# boost your energy

tired your digestion slows down and you don't absorb nutrients as efficiently as you should. Eat small but regular meals to sustain energy levels and keep blood sugar levels steady. It's easy to miss meals when you're busy so opt for healthy snacks such as fruit, brown pitta bread with hummus and vegetable sticks with cubes of cheese, rather than crisps and chocolate.

Certain nutrients can help boost flagging energy levels. Make sure you get sufficient amounts of B-group vitamins, particularly riboflavin, which converts carbohydrates into energy; vitamin $B_6$ essential for energy metabolism; and vitamin B12, required for forming red blood cells that carry oxygen throughout the body.

In some cases fatigue can be caused by a shortage of just one nutrient – iron. Depletion of this vital mineral reduces the amount of oxygen reaching the tissues. Women with heavy periods are especially vulnerable. Help your body absorb more iron by drinking a glass of orange juice once a day with a meal. Vitamin C also helps to boost energy. Other vital minerals include magnesium, which works with potassium and sodium to ensure the efficient working of muscles, along with zinc, which protects against viral infections that often precede chronic fatigue.

## USEFUL FOODS

- ✔ Shellfish, particularly oysters, are the richest source of zinc.
- ✔ Complex carbohydrate foods, wholemeal bread, pasta, wholegrain cereals and brown rice restore depleted energy levels.
- ✔ Meat and fish contain beneficial amounts of iron, as do green leafy vegetables, dried apricots, lentils and other pulses.
- ✔ Useful sources of B-group vitamins include wholegrains, chicken, fish, eggs, dairy produce, pulses, shellfish and red meat.

## AVOID

- ✖ Short-term energy boosters like caffeinated or sugary drinks cause energy levels to soar initially then plummet. Sugary foods, including biscuits, cakes and chocolate have a similar effect, leading to irritability and lethargy.
- ✖ Alcohol in large quantities is draining on body and mind – although the occasional glass of red wine can revive energy levels.
- ✖ Refined carbohydrate foods like white bread, pasta and rice destabilize energy levels by causing a sharp increase in blood sugar levels.

*Increase your energy levels with a seafood supper.*

**RECIPE**

## apricot purée

Dried apricots provide beneficial amounts of iron, beta carotene and vitamin C. This purée is very versatile: add a spoonful to natural live yogurt, use to fill tarts or serve with cooked meats. For an energizing breakfast, stir into porridge.

**Serves 2**

**Ingredients**

**175 g/6 oz dried unsulphured apricots, roughly chopped**

**1-cm/½-in piece fresh root ginger, finely grated (optional)**

**❶**

Place the apricots and ginger in a saucepan. Cover with water and bring to the boil. Reduce the heat and simmer for 10 minutes until soft.

**❷**

Allow to cool a little, then place the mixture, including the cooking liquid, in a food processor and purée until smooth.

*feeling great*

47

Sugary foods are one of the major causes of brain drain, feeding an inconsistent supply of energy to the brain that can actually 'cloud' mental activity.

The brain needs nourishment just like any other part of the body. Making positive changes to your diet will not only improve your physical health but also your mental well-being.

Diet influences the efficiency of the brain's chemical processes. Even a mild deficiency in just one nutrient can have a detrimental effect on memory, mental energy and concentration. Pineapples, pulses, nuts,

# memory enhancers

spinach and wholegrain cereals contain manganese, which aids poor memory by improving oxygenation and protecting brain tissue, while boron found in broccoli, nuts, apples, pears, grapes and pulses improves mental alertness. Zinc is a crucial brain mineral and is found in shellfish, dark turkey meat, wholegrains, beans, eggs and nuts. Oily fish, including herring, salmon, mackerel, tuna and sardines, is an excellent brain food, providing omega-3 essential fatty acids that are vital for the production of brain cells. Omega-6 fatty acids are also essential and are provided by vegetable oils, avocado, nuts and seeds.

The nutrient choline, also found in fish, is needed together with lecithin to produce the brain chemical acetylcholine, vital for the rapid functioning of memory. The amino acid tyrosine, found in milk, cheese and seafood, helps to increase mental energy and alertness. Protein foods in general nourish the brain and nervous system, whereas fruits and vegetables provide an abundance of brain nutrients, particularly antioxidants. The B-group vitamins, particularly riboflavin and thiamin, also stimulate brain cell energy and have been found to enhance memory. Eat wholegrains, nuts, seeds, meat, poultry, eggs and green vegetables on a regular basis.

## USEFUL FOODS

- ✔ Walnuts help to strengthen and nourish the brain since they are a source of both omega-3 and omega-6 essential fatty acids (EFAs) as well as B-group vitamins, iron, selenium, potassium and zinc. Other nuts and seeds offer similar benefits.
- ✔ Fish and shellfish are great brain foods, rich in omega-3, choline, zinc and B-group vitamins.
- ✔ Eggs are a complete protein, which means that they provide all the essential amino acids. They also contain choline, iron, selenium, zinc and vitamins A, D and E – a powerful brain combo.

## AVOID

- ✘ Sugary foods are one of the major causes of brain drain: they cause a temporary surge of blood glucose levels, followed by a slump. This leads to an inconsistent supply of energy to the brain that can actually 'cloud' mental activity.
- ✘ High-fat foods, especially those containing saturated and hydrogenated (trans) fats, can clog the arteries in the long term, thereby reducing the blood flow to the brain and affecting memory.
- ✘ Alcohol and smoking sap energy from the brain by damaging brain cells and inhibiting the absorption of vital minerals.

*Once at the centre of bad publicity, eggs provide a range of memory-enhancing nutrients.*

## honey-glazed salmon

This recipe provides a range of brain-boosting nutrients. Sprinkle with toasted sesame seeds to boost essential fatty acid levels and serve with brown rice and stir-fried broccoli.

**Serves 2**

**Ingredients**

2 x 150 g/5 oz salmon fillets, skinned

1 tbsp toasted sesame seeds

*Marinade*

1 garlic clove, crushed

2 tbsp runny honey

1 tbsp soy sauce

1 tbsp sunflower oil

1 tsp toasted sesame oil

 Mix together the ingredients for the marinade. Place the salmon in a shallow dish and pour the marinade over. Turn the fish to ensure it is completely covered. Leave to marinate in the refrigerator for at least 1 hour, turning the fish occasionally.

 Preheat the grill to high. Line the grill pan with foil and place the salmon on top. Brush the fish with the marinade and grill for about 6 minutes, turning once, until just cooked and still pink in the centre.

❸ Place the remaining marinade in a small saucepan and heat until thickened and reduced.

❹ Spoon the marinade over the salmon before serving and sprinkle with the sesame seeds.

 MEMORY TIPS

➕ THE HERBAL SUPPLEMENT GINKGO BILOBA BOOSTS SHORT-TERM MEMORY. GINSENG HAS SIMILAR BENEFITS, IMPROVING ALERTNESS AND CONCENTRATION, WHILE ALSO HELPING TO EASE FEELINGS OF STRESS AND DEPRESSION.

➕ MENTAL AND PHYSICAL EXERCISE BOTH HELP TO IMPROVE MEMORY. THE FORMER STIMULATES THE MIND WHILE AEROBIC EXERCISE INCREASES THE SUPPLY OF OXYGEN AND NUTRIENTS TO THE BRAIN.

➕ LACK OF SLEEP CAN DEPLETE EFFICIENCY OF THE BRAIN AND MEMORY; TRY TO GET THE HOURS YOU NEED.

*feeling great*

A nutrient-rich, balanced diet will make for an easier pregnancy as well as ensure good-quality breast milk and a quick postnatal recovery.

**E**ating a well-balanced diet throughout pregnancy is vital, not only for the mother-to-be but also for the health and development of the baby.

If you are planning to have a baby, good nutrition should be a priority, particularly since a poor diet can make conception difficult. If you are pregnant, now is the time to evaluate your diet and make any changes necessary to give your baby the best start in life. The first few weeks of

# pregnancy

pregnancy are crucial in nutritional terms. Don't restrict calories; nurture and nourish yourself and your developing child. Although you don't have to eat for two in terms of quantity, a nutrient-rich, balanced diet will make for an easier pregnancy as well as ensure good-quality breast milk and a quick postnatal recovery.

It is important to boost your intake of folic acid, ideally prior to but definitely in the early months of pregnancy, to avoid neural tube defects in the developing foetus, such as spina bifida. A specially formulated supplement (400mcg) is recommended by the Department of Health for the first 12 weeks, and eating the right foods will ensure you get sufficient amounts throughout the rest of your pregnancy. Iron-deficiency is common in pregnancy, so it is important to eat adequate amounts of lean red meat, dried apricots, eggs and green leafy vegetables. Zinc and calcium are equally important for the baby's growth. Magnesium-rich foods can prevent muscle cramps, while essential fatty acids found in fish, seeds and vegetable oil are vital for brain development. Try to eat a variety of fruits and vegetables to ensure sufficient intake of vitamins, minerals and fibre.

*healing foods*

*Vitamin C will help your body absorb the iron it needs.*

## USEFUL FOODS

- ✓ Folic acid, especially important pre-conception and in the first three months, is found in citrus fruits, pulses, green leafy vegetables, broccoli, dairy products, yeast extract and fortified cereals.
- ✓ Nuts, such as walnuts and almonds, as well as sunflower and pumpkin seeds, provide beneficial oils, zinc, calcium and magnesium.
- ✓ Omega-3 fatty acids, found in salmon, mackerel, herrings, sardines and tuna, are beneficial to a baby's brain development.
- ✓ Calcium-rich foods, including yogurt, milk, green leafy vegetables, tofu and sardines, will promote your baby's growth.

## AVOID

- ✗ Alcohol and caffeine prevent the absorption of zinc, low levels of which are linked to nerve abnormalities and low birth weight.
- ✗ Unpasteurized, blue or soft cheeses, soft eggs or undercooked meat and poultry present a risk of food poisoning, particularly listeriosis and salmonella.
- ✗ Foods containing high levels of vitamin A such as cod liver oil, liver and liver pâté can harm the foetus.
- ✗ Peanuts, including peanut oil-based creams, may trigger a reaction to nuts in your baby, especially if there is a history of nut allergy in your family.
- ✗ Smoking has been linked to an increased risk of miscarriage.

## watercress, orange & walnut salad

Beneficial oils, iron, beta carotene and vitamins C and E are provided by this simple, refreshing salad.

**Serves 2**

**Ingredients**

50 g/2 oz shelled walnuts, halved

75 g/3 oz watercress, tough stalks removed

1 large orange, peeled and sliced into thin rounds

*Dressing*

2 tsp lemon juice

½ tsp runny honey

1 tsp Dijon mustard

1½ tbsp extra virgin olive oil

salt and pepper

**❶**

Lightly toast the walnuts in a dry frying pan for 2 minutes until slightly golden. Toss them frequently to prevent burning. Leave to cool.

**❷**

To make the dressing, whisk the lemon juice, honey and mustard together in a bowl. Gradually whisk in the olive oil and season to taste with salt and pepper.

**❸**

Place the watercress, orange slices and walnuts in a salad bowl. Pour the dressing over and toss well with your hands before serving.

HRT offers many benefits, but it is not the only way to get through the menopause, and dietary changes can make a difference.

The menopause affects women in different ways, but for all it is a period of change, both mental and physical. Choosing the right foods can alleviate the range of symptoms associated with this time.

The menopause, when a woman's fertility gradually declines and childbearing years reach an end, usually begins around the age of 50, although it has been suggested that good nutrition and health may delay

# menopause

the onset. Symptoms vary from woman to woman: some breeze through with few problems, while others are blighted by hot flushes, insomnia, lack of libido, mood swings and depression. Hormone replacement therapy (HRT) offers many benefits, but it is not the only way to get through the menopause, and dietary changes can make a difference.

Calcium is vital to keep bones strong and healthy. Bone mass gradually declines during this time due to reduced levels of the hormone oestrogen. Vitamins C and D, boron, magnesium and zinc are also good for bone health. Numerous studies show that phytoestrogens found in various plant foods, such as soya beans, pulses, yams, linseeds and nuts can relieve many symptoms linked to the menopause, including hot flushes, by mimicking the hormone oestrogen. Oestrogen has an important role in regulating menstruation and protecting against osteoporosis. Vitamin E also reduces hot flushes.

Weight gain is common during the menopause, but is not inevitable. Stick to low-fat foods, while remembering that seeds, vegetable oils and oily fish can protect against heart disease, certain cancers and keep joints and the skin healthy. Zinc, magnesium, B-group vitamins and tryptophan can help with the common side effects of depression, mood swings and insomnia.

## USEFUL FOODS

- ✅ Soya-based foods such as tofu, soya beans and soya milk, which are rich in the plant substance phytoestrogens, can significantly reduce hot flushes.
- ✅ Sweet potatoes contain natural progesterone and can help with hormone imbalance.
- ✅ Calcium, in dairy products (stick to low-fat), wholegrains, green leafy vegetables, seeds, tofu, seaweed, white flour and sardines, helps keep bones strong.

## AVOID

- ❌ High-fat foods, especially those containing saturated or hydrogenated (trans) fats, increase the risk of heart disease and lead to weight gain.
- ❌ Alcohol, smoking, salty foods, animal protein, raw bran and saturated fat and foods containing oxalic acid, such as spinach and rhubarb, inhibit the intake of calcium.
- ❌ Caffeine also inhibits calcium absorption and can increase the intensity and regularity of hot flushes.

*Lentils are a good source of low-fat protein and provide valuable B vitamins.*

*healing foods*

## roasted chinese tofu

Rich in beneficial phytoestrogens, shown to alleviate hot flushes, tofu is best marinated before cooking since it has a neutral flavour. Serve this roasted tofu with stir-fried green vegetables and egg noodles.

**Serves 2**

**Ingredients**

225 g/8 oz tofu, cubed

*Marinade*

2 tbsp dark soy sauce or tamari

1 tsp vegetable oil

1 tsp toasted sesame oil

1 tbsp runny honey

2 garlic cloves crushed

2.5-cm/1-in piece fresh ginger, peeled and sliced

1 red chilli, deseeded and finely sliced

Combine all the ingredients for the marinade.

Place the tofu in a shallow dish and pour the marinade over. Carefully turn the tofu in the marinade making sure it doesn't break up and that all the pieces are coated. Marinate for at least 1 hour, turning the tofu in the marinade occasionally.

❸

Preheat the oven to 180°C/350°F/Gas Mark 4. Remove the tofu from the marinade using a slotted spoon and place on a baking tray. Bake for 20 minutes, turning occasionally, until golden and crisp on all sides.

❹

Strain the marinade into a small saucepan and bring to the boil. Reduce the heat and simmer until reduced and thickened. Spoon it over the tofu before serving.

## MENOPAUSE TIPS

⊕ A NUMBER OF HERBS HAVE BEEN SHOWN TO RELIEVE THE SYMPTOMS ASSOCIATED WITH THE MENOPAUSE: DONG QUAI FOR WATER RETENTION, HOT FLUSHES AND DRY SKIN; AGNUS CASTUS FOR HOT FLUSHES, LOST LIBIDO AND VAGINAL DRYNESS; BLACK COHOSH FOR HOT FLUSHES, IRRITABILITY AND INSOMNIA; AND ST JOHN'S WORT FOR MOOD SWINGS AND DEPRESSION.

*feeling great*

# →a-z nutritional healing

*The following guide explains how, by eating the right foods and avoiding the wrong ones, you can relieve a selection of the most common ailments and conditions, from acne and arthritis to osteoporosis and PMS. A helpful recipe accompanies the discussion of each condition, along with tips on complementary remedies that have helped other sufferers.*

Although there is no evidence that fatty food causes acne, a diet based on processed foods, sweets and snacks deprives the body of essential nutrients necessary for a healthy skin.

**S**tatistics show that 85 per cent of people between the ages of 12 and 25 suffer from acne in varying degrees. Dietary and lifestyle changes can play a crucial part in improving this skin condition.

Acne is triggered by hormonal changes at puberty and tends to affect more males than females – although spots are often more prevalent before menstruation. Genetic predisposition may be a factor, but dietary and

# acne

lifestyle choices certainly contribute. Although there is no evidence that fatty food in itself makes symptoms worse, a diet based on processed foods, sweets and snacks deprives the body of essential nutrients necessary for a healthy skin. Processed foods also tend to include a lot of salt, which has been found to aggravate acne. Try to avoid or cut back on salty foods, as well as seafood, which contain iodine, for 2–3 weeks to see if conditions improve.

A well-balanced, varied diet based on plenty of fresh fruits and vegetables, wholegrains, fish and some polyunsaturated oils is vital fuel for the skin. More specifically, zinc, B-group vitamins, beta carotene and vitamins C and E are essential. They also assist healing and help to reduce scarring. Including oily fish in the diet will similarly help the healing process and calm any inflammation. Water is vital, since it helps the body to flush out toxins.

Acne may be aggravated by food allergies and intolerances, especially to dairy products. Ask your doctor for advice, especially before eliminating foods from your diet. Stress depletes the skin of its natural defences, triggering a surge in hormones and an increase in the production of sebum, leading to an outbreak of spots. See pages 44–45 for advice on foods that can help to curb stress.

*Artichokes and beetroots have excellent skin-cleansing properties.*

## USEFUL FOODS

- Fresh fruits and vegetables are an excellent source of skin-boosting antioxidant vitamins C and E and also beta carotene.
- Natural live bio yogurt contains beneficial bacteria for a healthy digestive system, essential for blemish-free skin. (Antibiotics, often prescribed for acne, also kill 'good' bacteria in the gut.)
- Foods rich in zinc, such as shellfish, pumpkin seeds, lean meat, nuts, pulses and wholegrain bread, are vital for the skin.

## AVOID

- Milk should be kept to a minimum due its high hormone content.
- Refined sugar and fatty foods do not cause acne but if eaten in place of healthy, nutrient-rich foods can result in a deficient diet detrimental to the health of the skin.
- Processed and high-fat foods, which tend to contain high levels of salt, can contribute to acne.
- Ironically, seafood (see also Useful Foods) contains iodine, which can exacerbate acne.

### ACNE TIPS

➕ A DEFICIENCY IN THE DIGESTIVE ENZYMES RESPONSIBLE FOR BREAKING DOWN FATS MAY CAUSE ACNE. THE SUPPLEMENT LIPASE HELPS TO REBUILD DEPLETED LEVELS.

## RECIPE

### luxury muesli

This skin-nourishing muesli makes a perfect start to the day served with live natural bio yogurt and topped with sliced strawberries.

**Serves 6**

**Ingredients**

50 g/2 oz sunflower seeds

25 g/1 oz pumpkin seeds

25 g/1 oz sesame seeds

115 g/4 oz porridge oats

115 g/4 oz barley flakes

115 g/4 oz wheat flakes

115 g/4 oz raisins

115 g/4 oz roasted whole hazelnuts, chopped

75 g/3 oz almonds, roughly chopped

115 g/4 oz unsulphured dried apricots, roughly chopped

50 g/2 oz dried cherries

Lightly toast the sunflower, pumpkin and sesame seeds in a dry frying pan until just golden, tossing them regularly to prevent burning. Leave to cool.

Mix the toasted seeds with the rest of the ingredients. Store in an airtight container.

Studies show that a lack of vitamin C can contribute to osteoarthritis, but paradoxically, citrus fruits can exacerbate the symptoms.

**E**arly morning stiffness, pain and swelling of the joints, in varying degrees, are all symptoms of arthritis. Although there is no known cure, certain foods and diet can significantly alleviate the condition.

There are many forms of arthritis, the most prevalent being oesteoarthritis, a degenerative condition of the joints that causes stiffness and pain. Studies have found that a lack of antioxidant nutrients,

# arthritis

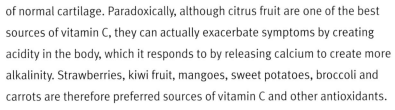

especially vitamin C, is one of the contributing factors. Vitamins A (beta carotene in plants), E and $B_6$ are also valuable, as are zinc and copper for the production of collagen and maintenance of normal cartilage. Paradoxically, although citrus fruit are one of the best sources of vitamin C, they can actually exacerbate symptoms by creating acidity in the body, which it responds to by releasing calcium to create more alkalinity. Strawberries, kiwi fruit, mangoes, sweet potatoes, broccoli and carrots are therefore preferred sources of vitamin C and other antioxidants.

Rheumatoid arthritis is a complex condition thought to be related to a malfunctioning immune system, resulting in severe pain and inflammation that eventually spreads throughout the joints. Recent studies show that the condition can be eased by a largely vegetarian diet based on wholefoods, fruits, vegetables, nuts, seeds and ginger, along with oily fish. An overall reduction in the intake of fat, processed foods, meat, sugar and refined carbohydrates may also help.

Food allergies and intolerances can aggravate arthritis, although you should consult your doctor before eliminating foods from the diet. Stress and lack of exercise are other contributors.

## USEFUL FOODS

- ✅ Pineapple contains bromelain, a helpful anti-inflammatory.
- ✅ Oily fish and cod liver oil have anti-inflammatory properties and can ease the pain of the condition.
- ✅ Flavonoid-rich berries such as cherries, blueberries and blackberries can help to relieve symptoms.
- ✅ Foods rich in the mineral boron, including lettuce, alfalfa, peas, cabbage, apples, almonds and hazelnuts, help the body to absorb calcium and have been found to ease the condition.
- ✅ Turmeric contains curcumin, an effective anti-inflammatory.

*Cherries are rich in flavonoids, an antioxidant that can bring relief to arthritis sufferers.*

## AVOID

- ❌ Members of the nightshade family of foods – aubergines, tomatoes, potatoes, peppers and tobacco – are all known irritants.
- ❌ Dairy products, corn, wheat, sugar, eggs, smoked and preserved foods, coffee and red meat are known to exacerbate rheumatoid arthritis.
- ❌ Sufferers of gout, another form of arthritis, should avoid alcohol, offal, game, poultry, shellfish and pulses since they are high in purines, which aggravate the condition.
- ❌ Animal sources of protein contain phosphorus and nitrogen, both of which make symptoms worse.

## pineapple & ginger crush

The anti-inflammatory combination of pineapple and ginger in this recipe can help to ease painful symptoms.

**Serves 2**

**Ingredients**

1 medium pineapple, peeled and cut into
　 slices

2.5-cm/1-in piece fresh ginger, peeled

crushed ice

Put the pineapple and ginger through a juicer. Pour over crushed ice and serve immediately.

### ARTHRITIS TIPS

✚ THE TOXIN-ELIMINATING YUCCA AND DEVIL'S CLAW CAN SUCCESSFULLY RELIEVE SYMPTOMS OF OSTEOARTHRITIS. GREEN-LIPPED MUSSEL EXTRACT, GLUCOSAMINE, AND COMPLEMENTARY THERAPIES LIKE ACUPUNCTURE, MASSAGE AND OSTEOPATHY, CAN ALSO BRING RELIEF.

*a–z nutritional healing*

Dark-green leafy vegetables, peas, figs, broccoli and courgettes provide magnesium, which is believed to protect against asthma by relaxing the muscles of the airways.

**E**xacerbated by poor air quality, pollution, and allergies to dust, animals and certain foods, respiratory problems are on the increase. A diet high in fresh fruits and vegetables may help relieve the symptoms.

Like other allergic conditions, including hayfever and eczema, asthma often runs in families. Recent studies, however, show a correlation between wheeziness and a diet lacking in fruits and vegetables.

# asthma

People who ate the most fresh produce were also found to have the healthiest lung function.

The beneficial effect of fruits and vegetables is attributed to their high antioxidant content. But fresh produce doesn't only play a preventative role: vitamin C along with other antioxidants, vitamin E and beta carotene have been shown to ease inflammation of the airways during an attack. Dark-green leafy vegetables, peas, figs, broccoli and courgettes are especially beneficial because they provide magnesium, which is believed to protect against asthma by relaxing the muscles of the airways.

Vitamin B$_6$ deficiency is common in asthmatics – avocados, sesame seeds, fish and poultry may help to reduce the severity of symptoms. Conversely, certain foods may trigger an asthma attack if the sufferer has an allergy or intolerance. These vary depending on the individual – a food that is tolerated by one asthma sufferer may cause an attack in another. A medically controlled allergy elimination diet will help to identify problematic foods. Some asthmatics also react to food additives, preservatives and colourings.

## USEFUL FOODS

- ✔ Fresh fruit provides a powerful combination of the antioxidants beta carotene and vitamin C, as well as fibre.
- ✔ Green leafy vegetables like broccoli, peas and courgettes are a good source of magnesium, fibre and antioxidant vitamins. Sunflower seeds, nuts, wholegrains, fish and soya also contain magnesium.
- ✔ Tomatoes, fresh and cooked, have been found to reduce the risk of asthma.

*Tomatoes are rich in lycopene, which promotes healthy lungs.*

- ✔ Onions, garlic, ginger and chilli can prevent an asthma attack by clearing the airways.
- ✔ The B-group vitamins, found in green leafy vegetables, pulses, lean meat, eggs, fish and dairy products may help asthmatics whose attacks are brought on by stress.

## AVOID

- ✘ Salt directly affects the muscles of the airways by constricting them. Reduction in salt intake may help to relieve symptoms.
- ✘ Preservatives known as 'sulphites', added to food such as dried fruit, squashes, wine, beer, cider, vinegar, sausages, burgers, jams and some

## gazpacho

This classic chilled soup contains
an abundance of fresh vegetables,
providing beneficial antioxidants.

**Serves 2**

**Ingredients**

1 slice day-old bread

450 g/1 lb vine-ripened tomatoes,
    peeled, deseeded and chopped

1 mini cucumber, peeled, deseeded and
    chopped

1 small red pepper, deseeded and
    chopped

1 green chilli, deseeded and sliced

1 garlic clove, crushed

1 tbsp extra virgin olive oil

juice of 1 lime

few drops Tabasco sauce

salt and pepper

½ avocado, peeled, deseeded and diced

squeeze of fresh lemon juice

4 ice cubes, to serve

**❶**

Soak the bread in a little water for
5 minutes. Place the bread with the
tomatoes, cucumber, red pepper, chilli,
garlic, oil, lime juice and Tabasco in a
food processor or blender. Add 250 ml/
8 fl oz water and blend until combined
but still chunky. Season to taste with
salt and pepper and chill for 2–3 hours.

**❷**

Just before serving toss the avocado in
the lemon juice. Ladle the soup into
bowls, add the ice cubes and top with
the avocado.

frozen vegetables, can bring on
attacks in susceptible people. The
food colourings tartrazine (E102),
quinoline yellow (E104) and sunset
yellow (E110) can also be a problem.

❌ Dairy products, wheat, red meat and
yeast may cause or aggravate the
symptoms of asthma.

❌ Foods containing histamine,
including strong sausages, ripe
cheese and some wines, can
trigger attacks in susceptible
people.

❌ Saturated fat and hydrogenated
(trans) fats may increase the
likelihood of asthma.

Antibiotics, stress, the pill, steroids and a diet high in refined sugars can all cause the candida micro-organism to multiply out of control.

Candida albicans is a yeast micro-organism that lives naturally in our bodies. This normally harmless yeast only causes problems when it multiplies out of control and becomes invasive.

Although candida is not fully understood, it is suggested that nearly one-third of the population in the Western world suffers from candida-related problems, namely

# candida

thrush, fatigue, depression, wind, headaches, bloating, allergies and food intolerances. Antibiotics, stress, the pill, steroids and a diet high in refined sugars typically cause the micro-organism to multiply out of control. Similarly, problems can occur after an infection or illness since the immune system is compromised.

When severe, candida flourishes in the gut, damaging, weakening and destroying 'good' bacteria. This is believed to affect the way nutrients are absorbed in the gut and leads to the release of harmful toxins into the body. If the gut and immune system are healthy, the good bacteria in the gut will keep the candida in check. Improving the internal flora of the gut is therefore vital to help curb the overgrowth of candida and subsequent problems. Live natural bio yogurt containing acidophilus cultures eaten on a regular basis is one way to help redress the balance.

Like all yeasts, candida feeds on sugar and starch and sufferers can experience a craving for these foods. Some alternative practitioners believe that people who suffer from recurrent candida-related problems should avoid all foods that contain sugar, yeast and moulds. Ask your GP or a dietician for advice.

## USEFUL FOODS

- ✓ Live natural bio yogurt contains 'good' bacteria that will improve the internal flora of your gut.
- ✓ Zinc-rich foods such as wholegrains, pulses, shellfish and red meat help to boost the immune system.
- ✓ The following foods have anti-fungal properties: onions, cabbage, broccoli, sprouts, kale, watercress, cauliflower, cinnamon and extra virgin olive oil.
- ✓ Vegetables rich in vitamin C, including broccoli, green leafy vegetables, tomatoes, spinach and peppers, help boost the immune system.

*Watercress has anti-fungal and immune-boosting properties that can help keep candida in check.*

## AVOID

- ✗ The following foods have been linked to candida overgrowth: all yeast-based foods such as leavened bread and pizza; alcohol; sugary foods, fruit juices (apart from freshly squeezed) and dried fruit; cheese; mushrooms and fungi of all kinds; pickled and fermented foods, including vinegar, soy sauce and relishes.

### CANDIDA TIPS

➕ PROBIOTIC SUPPLEMENTS, WIDELY AVAILABLE AT HEALTH FOOD SHOPS, CONTAIN BENEFICIAL BACTERIA THAT HELP TO IMPROVE THE CONDITION OF THE GUT.

**RECIPE**

## lentil & carrot soup

This nutritious soup makes a filling and wholesome lunch or supper. Serve with soda bread, which does not contain yeast, and a mixed green salad.

**Serves 2**

**Ingredients**

**1 tbsp olive oil**

**1 onion, chopped**

**2 garlic cloves, chopped**

**1 tsp each ground cumin, ginger and turmeric**

**2 carrots, sliced**

**115 g/4 oz red lentils**

**600 ml/1 pint vegetable stock**

**salt and pepper**

**2 tbsp live natural bio yogurt, to serve**

**❶**

Heat the oil in a saucepan, add the onion and fry for 8 minutes until softened. Add the garlic and spices and cook for 1 minute.

**❷**

Add the carrots and lentils and cook for 2 minutes, stirring continuously.

**❸**

Pour in the stock and bring to the boil. Reduce the heat and simmer for 40 minutes. Blend or process until smooth and creamy, adding more water if required. Season to taste with salt and pepper and serve with a spoonful of yogurt on top.

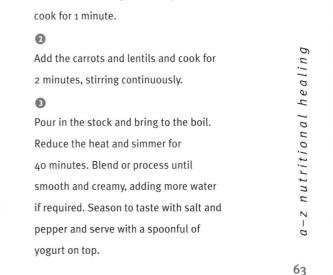

Constipation can normally be alleviated naturally: through drinking water, eating correctly and taking sufficient exercise.

**A** nutritionally balanced diet can go a long way to relieving most digestive problems, including constipation and irritable bowel syndrome (IBS).

Since the efficiency of our digestive system influences the successful absorption of nutrients from food, as well as affecting our long-term health and well-being, it essential to look after our insides. The most common digestive complaint is constipation, yet the problem can normally be

# constipation & ibs

alleviated completely naturally: through drinking plenty of water, eating correctly and taking sufficient exercise. Increasing your insoluble fibre intake is the first step, which is easily done by eating brown rice, whole-grain bread and pasta, dried and fresh fruits and vegetables. It is best to eat foods that are naturally high in fibre, rather than processed foods that have had fibre artificially added. Each person's fibre requirement varies, so experiment – too much can cause pain and bloating. Increase your intake gradually to prepare your body for the change. Dehydration can also aggravate constipation, so try to drink at least 6–8 glasses of filtered or mineral water a day.

The causes of IBS, characterized by abdominal pain, alternating bouts of constipation and diarrhoea, nausea and fatigue, are largely unknown, but the condition can be aggravated by food intolerance, too much fibre and stress. Choosing the right foods can help soothe the gut and increase its efficiency.

*Boost your fibre intake with nutritious dried apricots.*

## USEFUL FOODS

- ✓ Unrefined carbohydrates, including wholegrain bread, cereals, brown rice and pasta, as well as pulses and beans, are a good source of fibre and ease constipation.
- ✓ Fresh and dried fruits and vegetables also contain plentiful amounts of beneficial insoluble fibre.
- ✓ Natural live bio yogurt improves the condition of the gut and promotes good digestion.
- ✓ Peppermint tea and ginger tea may ease IBS.

## AVOID

- ✗ Refined carbohydrates, including white bread, pasta and rice, have a reduced fibre and nutrient content.
- ✗ Caffeine can help to counter constipation in the short-term, but it is also a diuretic, which means it makes you urinate more frequently, thereby leading to dehydration. IBS is also aggravated by caffeine.
- ✗ Alcohol and bran can exacerbate the symptoms of IBS.
- ✗ Intolerance to certain foods, particularly wheat and dairy, has been linked to IBS. Consult your doctor, however, before eliminating foods from your diet.

### WORD OF WARNING

✚ IF YOU HAVE A SENSITIVE GUT OR SUFFER FROM IRRITABLE BOWEL SYNDROME, YOU MAY FIND THAT LIVE YOGURT MAKES THE CONDITION WORSE. ASK YOUR DOCTOR FOR ADVICE.

## RECIPE

### exotic fruit salad

This refreshing combination of fruit not only tastes good but is an excellent source of fibre.

Serves 2–4

**Ingredients**

75 g/3 oz raspberries

1 small mango, peeled, stone removed and sliced

1 small pineapple, peeled, cored and thinly sliced

1 orange, peeled and thinly sliced

120 ml/4 fl oz fresh orange juice

1 tsp runny honey (optional)

**❶**

Purée the raspberries or press through a sieve. Place the purée in a serving bowl with the mango, pineapple and orange. Pour the orange juice over and stir to combine. Sweeten with honey.

Sweet foods can be eaten occasionally by diabetics but only after an unrefined starch meal or as part of a starchy food.

**D**ietary considerations are crucial in helping to control diabetes. This increasingly common condition occurs when the body loses its ability to regulate blood sugar levels.

There are two types of diabetes: insulin-dependent and non-insulin dependent. The first signs of diabetes are excessive thirst, frequent urination, weight loss, blurred vision and dizziness. People who are

# diabetes

insulin-dependent do not produce insulin themselves and require regular injections of the hormone, supported by a healthy diet and lifestyle. Those who are non-insulin dependent produce insufficient amounts of insulin or are unable to use what is produced in the body efficiently. This type is most common, particularly in middle-aged people who are overweight. The condition can be controlled by diet and regular exercise, and may also require medication.

If you have been diagnosed with diabetes, your doctor will advise you on an appropriate diet. Stick to a well-balanced intake of foods (see pages 8–13), namely plentiful amounts of fruits and vegetables, a moderate amount of wholegrains and pulses, nuts and seeds, animal protein and essential oils, small amounts of fat and minimal quantities of sugar. Sweet foods can be eaten occasionally by diabetics but only after an unrefined starch-based meal or as part of a starchy food, as the carbohydrate will keep blood sugar levels steady. Small regular meals, rather than three large meals a day, also help to keep blood sugar on an even keel. Special diabetic foods are unnecessary if you eat a carefully balanced diet.

## USEFUL FOODS

- ✓ Wholegrain starchy foods, including cereals, pasta and brown rice, help to maintain and stabilize blood sugar levels and provide steady amounts of energy. High-fibre foods also reduce harmful cholesterol in the body.
- ✓ Oily fish protect against heart disease, which is common among diabetics.
- ✓ Although fruit contains a type of sugar called fructose, its high fibre content helps to stabilize the release of the sugar into the bloodstream. Vegetables also provide valuable fibre.

## AVOID

- ✗ Refined carbohydrates like white bread, rice and pasta, and sugary foods like cakes, biscuits and sweets, cause sharp rises in blood sugar levels.
- ✗ Saturated fat and fried foods lead to weight gain, a common problem among diabetics. They also increase the risk of heart problems. Opt for low-fat sources of protein.
- ✗ Alcohol in large amounts is a risk. Enjoy in moderation, with a meal.
- ✗ Salt and salty foods increase the risk of high blood pressure, which is common amongst diabetics.

*Refined pasta can lead to a sharp increase in blood sugar. Unrefined pasta helps maintain and stabilize levels.*

## saffron chicken rice

Brown rice, chicken and fresh
vegetables are combined here to make a
simple, low-fat meal, providing useful
amounts of fibre, vitamins and minerals.
Serve with a green vegetable.

**Serves 2**

### Ingredients

1 onion, diced

1½ tbsp olive oil, plus extra
    for griddling

1 large skinless chicken breast, cut
    into cubes

1 small red pepper, deseeded and diced

2 garlic cloves, chopped

2 tomatoes, deseeded and chopped

2 tsp tomato purée

large pinch of saffron

500–550 ml/24 fl oz reduced-salt
    vegetable stock

150 g/6 oz brown rice

50 g/2 oz frozen peas

salt and pepper

**❶**

Fry the onion in the oil for 8 minutes in a
heavy-based sauté pan with a lid, until
softened. Add the pepper, garlic and
sauté for a further 3 minutes over a
medium heat.

**❷**

Add the tomato, tomato purée, saffron
and stock to the pan. Stir in the rice,
bring to the boil, then reduce the heat.
Cover, then simmer for 35 minutes or
until the rice is tender. Stir occasionally
and add extra stock or water, if required.

**❸**

Meanwhile, brush the chicken breast
with oil. Heat the griddle pan and cook

the chicken for 15–20 minutes, until
cooked through.

**❹**

Add the peas a minute before the end of
the rice cooking time. Season to taste
with salt and pepper. Place the rice in
serving bowls and top with the chicken,
cut into thin slices.

The sore, itchy, red rash of eczema is the body's way of eliminating perceived toxins. A varied, balanced diet will help boost your immune and digestive systems to strengthen the body's resistance.

**E**czema is becoming increasingly common, especially among children. Although it is difficult to treat, making certain dietary and lifestyle changes can bring relief.

Like hayfever and asthma, eczema can run in families and is often a reaction to allergies or intolerances, perhaps to food, or pets, dust mites, washing and cleaning detergents, or wool. It can be difficult to pinpoint

# eczema

the exact cause since it varies from one person to another. If you suffer with this condition, you should ask your GP to refer you to a skin specialist for allergy tests. Alternatively, a recommended naturopath or Chinese herbal practitioner may be able to help.

Dairy products, eggs and wheat are common food allergens. Tomatoes, citrus fruits, peanuts, food colourings and shellfish may also cause the characteristic sore, itchy, red rash of eczema, which is the body's way of eliminating what it sees as toxins. Stress can also aggravate the condition. It is important to boost the immune and digestive systems to strengthen the body's resistance to allergens and irritants; a varied, balanced diet containing plenty of fruit and vegetables will help.

Researchers have found that people with eczema lack the normal ability to process fats, which can result in a deficiency of gamma-linolenic acid (GLA), so supplementation may help. You can also boost the intake of beneficial oils through diet – oily fish, nuts, seeds and avocado all contain helpful polyunsaturated fats. Eczema sufferers are also often found to be lacking in the mineral zinc. However, some zinc-rich foods may also trigger eczema so it is crucial to monitor any variations in severity.

## USEFUL FOODS

- ✔ Salmon, tuna, herrings, mackerel, sardines and pilchards contain valuable omega-3 fatty acids.
- ✔ Zinc-rich foods may bring relief. Shellfish, grains, nuts, sunflower seeds, meat and dairy produce are good sources.
- ✔ Goat's, sheep's and soya milk are valuable alternatives to cow's milk and dairy products, which may trigger eczema.
- ✔ Green leafy vegetables, apples, onions, garlic and ginger are all excellent for the skin.

## AVOID

- ✘ Sugar has been found to aggravate eczema.
- ✘ Studies show that eczema sufferers who are heavy coffee drinkers can alleviate symptoms by cutting it out.
- ✘ Dairy products, eggs, wheat, tomatoes, fermented foods, shellfish, tea, chocolate, red meat, citrus fruits, peanuts and alcohol are common allergens. It may help to remove them from your diet, but consult your GP first.
- ✘ Food additives, histamines, colourings and also salicylates, used as preservatives and found naturally in many fruit and vegetables, may trigger the condition.

*The zinc found in nuts can bring relief to some eczema sufferers but exacerbate the condition in others.*

## baked oaty apples

Apples have a cleansing effect on the skin and, combined with the beneficial omega-6 oils found in sunflower seeds and zinc in oats, may bring relief to eczema sufferers.

**Serves 2**

**Ingredients**

2 large dessert apples, cored

40 g/1 ½ oz plain flour

2 tbsp unsalted butter or non-dairy
  alternative

2 tbsp whole oats

2 tbsp runny honey

1 tbsp sunflower seeds

55 g/2 oz dried dates, finely chopped

**❶**

Preheat the oven to 180°C/350°F/Gas Mark 4. Mix together the flour, butter, oats, honey, sunflower seeds and dates in a bowl. Fill the cavity of each apple with the oat mixture.

**❷**

Place the apples in an ovenproof dish and pour in a little water. Bake for 45 minutes or until the apples are tender.

### ECZEMA TIPS

✚ BORAGE, OIL, EVENING PRIMROSE OIL AND FISH OIL SUPPLEMENTS MAY RELIEVE ECZEMA, WHILE ECHINACEA BOOSTS THE IMMUNE SYSTEM, WHICH IS COMPROMISED IN PEOPLE SUSCEPTIBLE TO ALLERGIES. BOTH CALENDULA CREAM AND PURE SHEA BUTTER HAVE A SOOTHING, MOISTURIZING EFFECT ON THE SKIN, AND CAN HELP PREVENT CRACKING AND SCALINESS. THERE ARE ALSO A NUMBER OF RECOMMENDED HOMEOPATHIC REMEDIES. CONSULT A QUALIFIED HOMEOPATH, WHO WILL BE ABLE TO ADVISE ON A COURSE OF TREATMENT.

Fibre stays in the stomach for sustained periods, reducing the time the stomach is empty and consequently prone to acid attack. Try to eat a fibre-rich food at every meal.

**M**ost of us suffer from indigestion and heartburn at some time. Certain foods, eating habits and stress can trigger the condition, but making a few simple changes can make a big difference.

Indigestion caused by excessive acid in the stomach can be extremely painful and may be accompanied by belching and wind. If the acid is felt higher up in the chest and oesophagus, the feeding tube that leads from

# indigestion & heartburn

the mouth to the stomach, it is usually experienced as heartburn. Sufferers may also experience an acid taste in the mouth.

Indigestion and heartburn can strike when you have an empty stomach, after eating, or as a reaction to something eaten or drunk. Pregnant women often suffer as the growing baby in the uterus presses on the digestive tract. Although antacids have their place, they may lead to an overproduction of acid to compensate and can also interfere with the absorption of nutrients.

Foods containing fibre, including fruits, vegetables and wholegrains, are important. Fibre stays in the stomach for sustained periods, reducing the time the stomach is empty and consequently prone to acid attack. Try to eat a fibre-rich food at every meal but don't overdo it as too much can be hard to digest. Small, regular meals – every three to four hours – are advised to keep acid at bay. Try not to eat a large, fatty meal at night, but have something light instead, such as a simple soup, pasta, potato or rice dish. Eat slowly and avoid rushing around straight after a meal. Consult your GP if the problem persists.

*Fresh mint has a soothing, calming effect on the stomach and makes a refreshing tea.*

## RECIPE

The following infusions can help to soothe symptoms of indigestion and heartburn.

### mint tea

Place 3 tsp of chopped fresh mint leaves in a cup. Cover with boiling water and allow to infuse for a few minutes. Serve warm after a meal.

### ginger tea

Slice a 2.5-cm/1-inch piece of fresh ginger and place in a cup. Cover with boiling water and allow to infuse for 3 minutes before serving warm. This tea is also good for nausea.

### camomile tea

Use a tea bag or place 2 tsp of dried camomile in a cup. Cover with boiling water. Infuse for 3 minutes before sipping.

### INDIGESTION TIPS

✛ STRESS MAY EXACERBATE INDIGESTION, SO RELAXATION TECHNIQUES COULD HELP. LAVENDER, ROSE, MINT AND GINGER AROMATHERAPY OILS CAN ALL HELP YOU TO RELAX. ADD A FEW DROPS TO THE BATH OR COMBINE WITH A CARRIER OIL AND MASSAGE INTO THE BODY.

*a–z nutritional healing*

Eating a large meal late in the evening can interfere with sleep patterns. Try to leave 2–3 hours between eating and going to bed.

There is evidence to suggest that what you eat and drink, particularly before bedtime, can determine whether you get a good night's rest.

Up to a third of adults in the UK suffer from some form of insomnia, and as many as half say they are dissatisfied with the quality of their sleep. Insomnia is frustrating, exhausting and can take its toll both emotionally and physically. A good night's sleep makes you feel rejuvenated, more relaxed and better able to cope.

# insomnia

Stress, depression, anxiety, as well as pregnancy and the menopause, can all disrupt sleep patterns, but diet may also play a role. Consider your eating patterns – keeping a food diary will help you discover whether certain meals or dietary habits directly influence your sleep. Eating a large meal late in the evening, for example, can interfere with sleep patterns. The digestive system is not as efficient at night and a large, rich or spicy meal puts an extra burden on the body. Try to leave 2–3 hours between eating and going to bed.

Conversely, going to bed on an empty stomach may cause you to wake during the night. A meal based on carbohydrate foods, such as pasta, rice or potatoes, with a small amount of protein in the form of chicken, fish, lean meat or pulses is the perfect balance for sleep, while too much protein and sugar may have the opposite effect. Carbohydrates, particularly the unrefined sort, help to maintain blood sugar levels and increase the level of the neurotransmitter serotonin in the brain, which encourages sleep.

72

## USEFUL FOODS

✔ A light snack such as a banana, wholemeal muffin or toast, flapjack or glass of warm milk will keep blood sugar levels steady throughout the night and boost serotonin levels.

✔ Unrefined carbohydrates like wholemeal bread and brown rice and pasta will lead to a better night's sleep than the refined, white alternatives.

✔ Herbal teas, particularly camomile, have a soothing, calming influence.

✔ Wholegrains, seafood, eggs, poultry, nuts, beans, lentils and dairy foods are a good source of B vitamins, which may influence sleep and play a role in regulating serotonin levels.

*Eggs contain tryptophan, which helps in the production of the brain-calming chemical serotonin.*

## AVOID

✘ Coffee, tea, cola and drinking chocolate all contain the stimulant caffeine, which causes insomnia and dehydration.

✘ One or two alcoholic drinks may aid relaxation, but too many can interfere with sleep patterns and cause dehydration.

✘ Sugar causes a surge in blood sugar levels that will keep you awake.

✘ Spicy and high-fat foods, such as cheese, put a strain on the digestive system, particularly if eaten too close to bedtime.

## RECIPE

### speedy tuna pasta

Pasta, particularly wholemeal, combined with tuna encourages the production of the sleep-inducing serotonin in the brain.

**Serves 2**

**Ingredients**

150 g/5 oz wholemeal spaghetti

1 tbsp olive oil

1 garlic clove, chopped

120 ml/4 fl oz white wine (optional)

300 ml/½ pint passata

pinch of sugar (optional)

1 tsp dried oregano

small tin tuna fish in oil, drained

salt and pepper

Cook the pasta according to the packet instructions. Drain, reserving a little of the cooking water. Meanwhile, heat the oil in a heavy-based saucepan. Fry the garlic for 1 minute. Pour in the wine, if using, and boil until reduced and the alcohol has evaporated.

❷
Reduce the heat and add the passata, sugar and oregano and cook for a further 10 minutes. Add the tuna and cooking water, season with salt and pepper, and cook for another 5 minutes.

❸
Top the pasta with the sauce and serve.

Both headaches and migraines can occur when blood sugars are out of kilter, swinging from very low to very high and vice versa.

**B**oth headaches and migraines can be debilitating, and the point where a headache becomes a migraine is unclear. What is evident is that diet can have an influence.

Stress, anxiety, dehydration, alcohol, certain foods and poor eating habits can all contribute to headaches and migraines. Migraines come with a range of symptoms from severe headache, nausea and vomiting to

# migraines & headaches

blurred and disturbed vision, which may include flashing or zigzag lights before the eyes and a dislike of bright light. They tend to affect more women than men and can be triggered by a number of factors, one of which is diet.

It's a good idea to keep a food diary for a few weeks to determine whether there is a pattern to your migraines. Eating small, regular meals and avoiding certain foods may be sufficient to curb symptoms. Both headaches and migraines can occur when blood sugars are out of kilter, swinging from very low to very high and vice versa. To even out these irregularities, avoid refined sugary foods and, if you fancy something sweet, make sure it contains some fibre so that you experience a steady rise in blood sugar – dried fruit, bananas, oatcakes with jam, flapjacks, for example. Avoid skipping meals as this will cause a dip in blood sugar.

Foods rich in magnesium as well as oily fish have been found to help prevent migraines and headaches. Food allergies have also been implicated as a trigger: ask your doctor for a referral to a specialist dietician to rule out this cause.

*Magnesium-rich foods, including nuts, can help prevent a migraine attack.*

*healing foods*

## USEFUL FOODS

- ✔ High-fibre foods, including wholegrain bread, oatcakes, brown rice, fruit and vegetables and wholemeal pasta help to keep blood sugar levels steady.
- ✔ Magnesium-rich foods – nuts, seeds, wholegrains, green vegetables and soya – can help to prevent migraines.
- ✔ Oily fish – sardines, mackerel, salmon, herrings and tuna – are also believed to help prevent migraines as they have an anti-inflammatory effect.
- ✔ Make sure you drink plenty of water, as dehydration causes headaches.

## AVOID

- ✘ Chocolate, hard cheese, sour cream, red wine, smoked and cured fish and meat contain substances that can trigger a migraine.
- ✘ Caffeine can set off a migraine, so cut down on coffee, tea and cola – but do it gradually as a dramatic withdrawal can also trigger an attack.
- ✘ Food additives, including artificial sweeteners, nitrates in preserved meat as well as monosodium glutamate (MSG) used in crisps, bottled sauces, ready-meals and by some Chinese restaurants, can trigger migraines and headaches.

## RECIPE

### mixed herb salad with toasted nuts and seeds

This salad contains beneficial vitamins, minerals and oils, and makes a perfect light lunch served with crusty wholemeal bread.

Serves 2

**Ingredients**

50 g/2 oz mixed salad leaves, including watercress and spinach

50 g/2 oz mixed herbs, including parsley, rocket and basil

1 tbsp sunflower seeds

1 tbsp pumpkin seeds

1 tbsp pine nuts

*Dressing*

2 tbsp extra virgin olive oil

1–2 tsp fresh lemon juice

salt and pepper

**❶**

Arrange the salad leaves and herbs in a serving bowl. Lightly toast the seeds and pine nuts in a dry frying pan until just coloured. Leave them to cool slightly before sprinkling over the salad.

**❷**

Mix together the olive oil and lemon juice. Season to taste with salt and pepper and drizzle over the salad.

### MIGRAINE TIPS

✚ HEADACHES AND MIGRAINES ARE OFTEN CAUSED BY STRESS. MASSAGE LAVENDER ESSENTIAL OIL INTO YOUR TEMPLES AND TRY RELAXATION TECHNIQUES, MEDITATION AND YOGA TO RELIEVE TENSION.

Evidence suggests that eating more calcium-rich foods from a young age will help to prevent or slow down the onset of osteoporosis.

**W**hat you eat has a huge influence on the condition and strength of your bones. The best approach to maintaining good bone health is a balanced diet combined with regular weight-bearing exercise.

The key years for the formation of a healthy skeleton are between puberty and 30, when bone mass reaches a peak and then begins to level off. With advancing age, the bones of both women and men become

# osteoporosis

progressively weaker and prone to fracture. Women are more vulnerable due to their smaller frames and declining levels of the hormone oestrogen and subsequent calcium loss during the menopause. Excessive dieting, especially during the key years, has a detrimental effect on the skeleton, since the body is starved of the nutrients required for bone health. Dieting can also interfere with oestrogen production in women.

There is growing evidence to suggest that eating more calcium-rich foods from a young age will help to prevent or slow down the onset of osteoporosis. Adequate levels of vitamin D are also essential for the absorption of calcium. Getting outdoors in the sunshine helps the skin to make this nutrient, which is also found in some foods. Magnesium, boron, zinc, manganese and copper are also needed for good bones. If you eat a well-balanced, varied diet you should be getting sufficient quantities of all these nutrients.

Regular exercise is just as important for building bone strength, since it ensures nutrients are more readily absorbed where they are needed and encourages new bone formation. Jogging, aerobics and walking are all recommended.

## USEFUL FOODS

- ✔ Milk, cheese, yogurt and fromage frais are good sources of calcium. Opt for low-fat versions, which contain as much of the mineral as their full-fat counterparts.
- ✔ Soya beans, soya milk and tofu, green leafy vegetables, fortified cereals, sardines and sesame seeds also provide calcium.
- ✔ Food sources of vitamin D include margarine, butter, oily fish, fortified cereals and eggs.
- ✔ Wholegrains, nuts, seeds, dried apricots and green vegetables are a good source of valuable magnesium.

## AVOID

- ✘ Salt intake should be reduced in those vulnerable to osteoporosis as it increases calcium loss.
- ✘ Smoking and alcohol reduce calcium absorption, encourage its loss and accelerate bone weakness. Smoking also interferes with oestrogen production.
- ✘ The phosphorus in fizzy drinks is believed to alter the balance of minerals in the body if drunk in excess, encouraging it to release calcium from the bones.
- ✘ A high intake of animal protein can increase calcium loss in the body.

*The humble cabbage contains magnesium, which is important for strong bones.*

## sardines on toast

This simple snack provides plentiful amounts of the nutrients necessary for good health.

**Serves 1**

**Ingredients**

2 slices wholemeal bread

butter or margarine, for spreading

1 can sardines in olive oil

1 tomato, deseeded and chopped

sprinkling of dried chilli flakes

salt and pepper

1 tbsp chopped fresh parsley, to garnish

**❶**

Preheat the grill to high. Toast both slices of bread on one side. Spread lightly with butter or margarine.

**❷**

Drain the sardines and arrange them on top of the untoasted sides of the bread. Top with the chopped tomato and a few dried chilli flakes. Season to taste with salt and pepper. Grill for 3 minutes until golden. Sprinkle with parsley before serving.

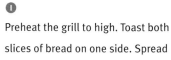

## OSTEOPOROSIS TIPS

✚ CALCIUM AND BONE HEALTH SUPPLEMENTS ARE RECOMMENDED FOR MENOPAUSAL AND POST-MENOPAUSAL WOMEN, AND ALSO REGULAR DIETERS.

Certain foods and dietary habits can aggravate or sometimes even cause PMS. Keep a food diary to monitor your moods and physical changes throughout the month.

# pms

**M**aking some simple changes to your diet can help alleviate many of the symptoms associated with premenstrual syndrome (PMS).

Premenstrual syndrome is the term used to describe a collection of symptoms, physical and emotional, that occur prior to menstruation and are usually related to changing hormone levels. Symptoms vary depending on the individual but may include irritability, mood swings and forgetfulness, tender breasts, cravings and cramp – and many more besides. Most commonly, symptoms begin a few days before a period starts and diminish when it begins.

Certain foods and dietary habits can aggravate or sometimes even cause PMS. You may find it useful to keep a food diary to monitor your moods and physical changes throughout the month. The principles of a well-balanced, varied diet apply here. Eat plenty of fruits and vegetables, high-fibre unrefined starches, moderate amounts of protein foods such as fish, eggs, cheese and meat and drink at least 6–8 glasses of mineral or filtered water a day.

Deficiencies in vitamin $B_6$ and vitamin E, zinc and magnesium have been detected in those suffering from PMS, symptoms of which are irritability, fatigue and mood swings. Mood swings and fatigue can also be caused by erratic blood sugar levels. Try eating a carbohydrate-rich snack during the last two weeks of your cycle. Symptoms of PMS may also be aggravated by food intolerances and candida. If you believe either of these may be a factor, it is important to seek the advice of your GP.

## PMS TIPS

➕ SEVERAL SUPPLEMENTS HAVE BEEN SHOWN TO HELP TREAT PMS, INCLUDING EVENING PRIMROSE OIL, VITAMIN $B_6$, MAGNESIUM AND CALCIUM.

## USEFUL FOODS

✓ Vitamin $B_6$, which is sometimes deficient in PMS sufferers, is found in green leafy vegetables, bananas, nuts, poultry, wholegrains and oily fish.

✓ Snacks such as wholemeal toast, muffins, pitta bread, cereal bars, flapjacks or bananas help to keep blood sugar levels steady and prevent mood swings and fatigue.

✓ Foods rich in vitamin E such as avocado, eggs, wheatgerm and cold-pressed oils may help to reduce breast tenderness.

✓ Magnesium-rich foods, including wholegrains, shellfish, nuts and dried fruit, are important inclusions in the diet of the PMS sufferer.

*The vitamin E in avocados can help to relieve breast tenderness.*

## AVOID

✗ Caffeine inhibits the absorption of certain nutrients and can contribute to anxiety and mood swings.

✗ Sugar and processed foods like cakes, biscuits, chocolate, fizzy drinks and puddings lack nutrients, destabilize blood sugar levels and may cause water retention.

✗ Salt and salty foods contribute to PMS and cause water retention.

✗ Alcohol and smoking will only aggravate the symptoms.

✗ Cut down on fats, particularly saturated and hydrogenated (trans) fats found in processed foods.

## RECIPE

## chicken, avocado & rocket wrap

This nutritious snack can be turned into a main meal if served with a salad and new potatoes.

**Serves 1**

### Ingredients

1 small avocado

1 small garlic clove, crushed

squeeze fresh lemon juice

1 tsp low-fat mayonnaise

1 tortilla wrap

1 small cooked, preferably roasted, chicken breast, sliced on the diagonal

handful wild rocket leaves

salt and pepper

Roughly mash the avocado with the garlic, lemon juice and mayonnaise. Gently warm the tortilla and spread with the avocado mixture.

❷

Arrange the chicken and rocket leaves on top. Season and roll up before serving.

# →healing foods
## directory

*Use the Directory to identify the foods that are best suited to your particular needs, to find out the nutrients they contain, how they can help and heal, and when they should be avoided. This information will arm you with the means to make positive changes to your diet.*

| FOOD | NUTRIENTS | HELPS & HEALS | TIPS |
|---|---|---|---|
| **Apple** | ⊃ Vitamin C<br>⊃ Potassium<br>⊃ Fibre | ⊕ Removes impurities in the liver<br>⊕ Aids digestion and encourages natural beneficial bacteria to thrive in the digestive tract<br>⊕ Good for skin, rheumatism, circulation and arthritis if eaten regularly<br>⊕ Effective detoxifier and pick-me-up | ❶ Look for firm, unbruised fruit. Try to buy locally grown, in season |
| **Alfalfa** | ⊃ Vitamins A & D<br>⊃ Complete protein<br>⊃ Calcium & phosphorus<br>⊃ Iron<br>⊃ Potassium | ⊕ One of the most nutritionally rich foods, valued for its ability to cleanse and rejuvenate the system<br>⊕ Anti-inflammatory and aids digestion<br>⊕ Boosts the immune system and relieves arthritis, rheumatism and bloating | ❶ Avoid if you suffer from rheumatoid arthritis<br>❶ Avoid buying mushy, old sprouts. Best eaten raw. Why not try sprouting your own? |
| **Apricot** | ⊃ Beta carotene<br>⊃ Vitamin C<br>⊃ Iron (particularly when dried)<br>⊃ Magnesium<br>⊃ Potassium & boron | ⊕ Good for infections of the respiratory system<br>⊕ Antioxidant qualities may help to reduce risk of heart disease and certain cancers<br>⊕ Laxative<br>⊕ Helps prevent high blood pressure and fight fatigue<br>⊕ May help to prevent osteoporosis | ❶ Look for dried apricots that have not been preserved in sulphur dioxide, which can trigger asthma attacks in susceptible people |
| **Artichoke** | ⊃ Folate<br>⊃ Vitamin C<br>⊃ Potassium | ⊕ Aids the digestion process; diuretic<br>⊕ Protects and regenerates the liver, particularly the leaf<br>⊕ Reduces cholesterol levels, protecting against heart disease<br>⊕ Purifying and detoxifying | ❶ Look for artichokes with tightly packed, firm leaves with the stalk intact |
| **Asparagus** | ⊃ Folate<br>⊃ Fibre<br>⊃ Vitamin C<br>⊃ Vitamin E | ⊕ Diuretic and mildly laxative<br>⊕ Good for the kidneys, liver, skin and bones<br>⊕ Contains the antioxidant glutathione, said to prevent the formation of cataracts | ❶ Avoid if suffering from gout<br>❶ Look for tender, young stems with firm stalks. Eat within 2–3 days of purchase |

| FOOD | NUTRIENTS | HELPS & HEALS | TIPS |
|---|---|---|---|
| **Avocado** | ◉ Iron<br>◉ Good source of monounsaturated fats<br>◉ Vitamins C & E<br>◉ Beta carotene<br>◉ Potassium & manganese | ⊕ Improves condition of skin and hair<br>⊕ Soothes digestive tract<br>⊕ Good for anaemia<br>⊕ Beneficial fats help to reduce blood cholesterol<br>⊕ Helps stress and depression | ❶ Look for almost ripe fruit and store at room temperature until softened. Store ripe fruit in the refrigerator<br>❶ Brush with lemon juice when cut to prevent discolouration |
| **Banana** | ◉ Potassium<br>◉ Fibre<br>◉ Zinc<br>◉ Iron<br>◉ Folate<br>◉ Vitamin B$_6$ | ⊕ Rich in the amino acid tryptophan, known to lift the spirits and aid sleep<br>⊕ Aids functioning of cells, nerves and muscles<br>⊕ Eases high blood pressure<br>⊕ Soothes the stomach and digestive system, relieving both constipation and diarrhoea<br>⊕ Boosts energy levels<br>⊕ Helps the body eliminate toxins | ❶ Eat ripe fruit; green bananas are difficult to digest and cause intestinal wind |
| **Basil** | ◉ Trace calcium, magnesium and manganese | ⊕ Aids digestion and helps relieve colic and wind<br>⊕ Rub basil leaves on insect bites to soothe irritation and prevent infection<br>⊕ Believed to help clear the mind<br>⊕ Stimulates appetite and counteracts nausea | ❶ Add some fresh leaves to your bath for an uplift |
| **Beetroot** | ◉ Vitamins A, B & C<br>◉ Calcium<br>◉ Iron<br>◉ Potassium & magnesium<br>◉ Folate | ⊕ General tonic; supports the immune system<br>⊕ Detoxifies the liver, gallbladder and kidneys<br>⊕ Maintains normal blood pressure and combats anaemia | ❶ Particularly beneficial when freshly boiled |
| **Blackcurrant** | ◉ Vitamin C<br>◉ Vitamin E<br>◉ Beta carotene<br>◉ Fibre | ⊕ Contains pigments called anthocyanins, which are anti-inflammatory and antibacterial<br>⊕ Soothes sore throats<br>⊕ Eases stomach upsets<br>⊕ Antioxidant qualities help to protect against heart disease, strokes and certain cancers | ❶ Look for firm, glossy berries. Ripe blackcurrants do not keep well so eat soon after purchase |

| FOOD | NUTRIENTS | HELPS & HEALS | TIPS |
|------|-----------|---------------|------|
| **Blueberry** | ➡ B VITAMINS<br>➡ FIBRE<br>➡ VITAMIN C | ➕ Memory enhancer<br>➕ Helps combat cystitis and other urinary tract infections<br>➕ Detoxifier and antioxidant with anti-infection and anti-inflammatory properties<br>➕ Benefits eyesight; may improve night and light vision; prevent cataracts<br>➕ Improves circulation, helping to prevent broken and varicose veins | ❶ Like other berries, blueberries may trigger allergies |
| **Broccoli** | ➡ VITAMINS C, E, B5<br>➡ BETA CAROTENE<br>➡ FOLATE<br>➡ IRON & ZINC<br>➡ POTASSIUM<br>➡ CALCIUM | ➕ Protects against cancer of the lung, colon and breast<br>➕ Inhibits the spread of certain cancers<br>➕ High in antioxidants, so helps to reduce the risk of heart disease and strokes<br>➕ Antibacterial and antiviral | ❶ Lightly steam or add raw to salads to retain the valuable nutrients of this super-veg |
| **Cabbage** | ➡ VITAMINS C & E<br>➡ FIBRE<br>➡ BETA CAROTENE<br>➡ FOLATE<br>➡ POTASSIUM<br>➡ IRON<br>➡ MAGNESIUM | ➕ Raw cabbage juice hastens the healing of stomach and duodenal ulcers<br>➕ Anti-carcinogenic cocktail – reduces the risk of stomach, lung, skin, breast, womb and colon cancer<br>➕ High antioxidant levels reduce the risk of heart disease and strokes<br>➕ Prevents anaemia and protects against stress and infection<br>➕ Detoxifies the stomach | ❶ Apply dark-green leafy varieties (Savoy) externally to soothe leg ulcers, wounds and mastitis |
| **Carrot** | ➡ BETA CAROTENE<br>➡ VITAMINS C & B<br>➡ FIBRE<br>➡ CALCIUM<br>➡ IRON<br>➡ POTASSIUM | ➕ Helps prevent and treat cancer of the lung, prostate, bladder, cervix, colon and oesophagus<br>➕ Excellent detoxifier, cleansing and nourishing every system of the body<br>➕ Promotes healthy vision, skin and bones<br>➕ Aids the respiratory and digestive system<br>➕ Helps ward off colds<br>➕ Reduces the risk of heart disease and strokes due to its antioxidant qualities | ❶ Surprisingly, carrots are more nutritious when lightly cooked than raw as their vitamins and minerals are more readily assimilated |
| **Chilli** | ➡ VITAMIN C<br>➡ BETA CAROTENE<br>➡ VITAMIN E<br>➡ FOLATE | ➕ Stimulates circulation and helps prevent blood clots<br>➕ Eases coughs and colds, clearing congestion<br>➕ May protect the stomach against alcohol and acidic food<br>➕ Anticoagulant – helps to reduce blood pressure and cholesterol levels<br>➕ Stimulates the release of endorphins, the body's 'feel-good' chemicals | ❶ May irritate the stomach if eaten in excess |

| FOOD | NUTRIENTS | HELPS & HEALS | TIPS |
|---|---|---|---|
| **Cranberry** | → Vitamin C<br>→ Beta carotene<br>→ Potassium<br>→ Iron | ⊕ Helps prevent and treat urinary tract infections, particularly cystitis<br>⊕ Antifungal, antibacterial and antiviral<br>⊕ May help people with kidney stones | ❶ Shop-bought cranberry juice can be high in sugar, making it unsuitable for diabetics |
| **Dates** | → Vitamin C<br>→ Potassium<br>→ Fibre<br>→ Iron | ⊕ Gentle laxative<br>⊕ Energizing and nourishing fruit, useful for convalescents | ❶ The natural sugar content of dates is preferable to refined white sugar but can still cause tooth decay<br>❶ Tyramine content may trigger migraines |
| **Egg** | → Iron<br>→ B vitamins<br>→ Vitamins A & E<br>→ Selenium<br>→ Zinc<br>→ Good source of protein | ⊕ Antioxidant qualities may help to protect against some forms of cancer<br>⊕ One of the few sources of vitamin B12 – essential for the nervous system – for vegetarians | ❶ Children, pregnant women, the sick and elderly should avoid raw or under-cooked eggs<br>❶ Although eggs are high in cholesterol, a diet high in saturated fat plays a bigger role in raising cholesterol level in the body |
| **Flaxseed** | → Omega-3 fatty acids<br>→ Vitamin E<br>→ Iron<br>→ Calcium<br>→ Potassium<br>→ Magnesium | ⊕ Also known as linseed, flaxseed is one of the best vegetarian sources of omega-3 fatty acids. Protects against heart disease and some forms of cancer, particularly breast<br>⊕ Relieves constipation and soothes digestion<br>⊕ Eases menopausal symptoms | ❶ Sprinkle golden linseeds over salads and breakfast cereals |
| **Garlic** | → Sulphur<br>→ Iodine | ⊕ Wonder food with anti-cancer, antiviral, antibacterial and antifungal qualities<br>⊕ Protects the heart by helping to reduce blood cholesterol levels and blood pressure; prevents blood clots by thinning the blood<br>⊕ Good for sinus and chest infections, colds and flu<br>⊕ Can help diabetics by reducing blood sugar levels | ❶ Studies show that eating 2–3 cloves of garlic a day halves the risk of a subsequent heart attack in previous heart patients |

*healing foods directory*

| FOOD | NUTRIENTS | HELPS & HEALS | TIPS |
|---|---|---|---|
| **Ginger** | ➲ Potassium<br>➲ Calcium<br>➲ Iron<br>➲ Magnesium | ➕ Aids digestion and is an effective remedy for nausea<br>➕ Effective against colds, flu and chest congestion<br>➕ Reduces the risk of blood clots<br>➕ Stimulates circulation and cleanses the system | ❶ Steep slices of fresh ginger in hot water and sip to fight a cold or soothe sickness |
| **Grapes** | ➲ Vitamin C<br>➲ Iron (particularly in black grapes)<br>➲ Potassium<br>➲ Fibre | ➕ Powerful antioxidant flavonoids help protect against heart disease and certain cancers<br>➕ Powerful detoxifier, so improves the condition of the skin<br>➕ Treats gout as well as liver and kidney disorders<br>➕ Nourishing and strengthening qualities make grapes useful for convalescents as well as those with fatigue and anaemia | ❶ Wash grapes thoroughly as they are routinely sprayed with pesticides – or buy organic<br>❶ May trigger migraines |
| **Green Tea** | ➲ Quercetin (an antioxidant) | ➕ The polyphenols in green tea help to protect against heart disease by reducing cholesterol levels, blood pressure and risk of blood clots<br>➕ May protect against some forms of cancer, including stomach<br>➕ Antiviral qualities protect against flu | ❶ Black tea has similar therapeutic properties but to a slightly lesser degree |
| **Honey** | ➲ Potassium<br>➲ Magnesium<br>➲ Phosphorus | ➕ Wound-healing properties if used externally<br>➕ Antiseptic and antibacterial: soothes digestive problems and sore throats<br>➕ Cold-pressed honey may protect against hay fever | ❶ Do not give to babies under 1 year<br>❶ Raw, cold-pressed honey has the best healing properties |
| **Lentils** | ➲ B vitamins<br>➲ Fibre<br>➲ Iron<br>➲ Zinc<br>➲ Potassium | ➕ Reduces blood cholesterol levels and regulates high blood pressure, protecting against heart disease<br>➕ Aids functioning of bowels and colon<br>➕ Fibre helps to control blood sugar levels<br>➕ Fights fatigue, anaemia and poor memory | ❶ Lentils are high in purines and should therefore be avoided by people with gout |

| FOOD | NUTRIENTS | HELPS & HEALS | TIPS |
|---|---|---|---|
| **Nuts** | ➲ VITAMINS B & E<br>➲ MAGNESIUM & MANGANESE<br>➲ ZINC<br>➲ IRON<br>➲ SELENIUM | ⊕ Essential fatty acids (found especially in walnuts, almonds and hazelnuts) may protect against heart disease and reduce the risk of strokes. Also vital for tissue development and growth<br>⊕ Vitamin E content reduces the risk of certain cancers | ❶ Nuts contain high amounts of fat, although it is largely monounsaturated. Eat in moderation |
| **Oats** | ➲ VITAMINS B & E<br>➲ IRON<br>➲ CALCIUM<br>➲ MAGNESIUM<br>➲ FIBRE | ⊕ Effectively reduces blood cholesterol, increasing beneficial HDL cholesterol levels<br>⊕ Eases constipation<br>⊕ May calm the nerves<br>⊕ Helps stabilize blood sugar levels, so useful for diabetics | ❶ Porridge oats for breakfast make an excellent start to the day |
| **Oily Fish** | ➲ OMEGA-3 ESSENTIAL FATTY ACIDS<br>➲ VITAMINS E & D<br>➲ ZINC<br>➲ CALCIUM<br>➲ IRON<br>➲ IODINE | ⊕ Essential for healthy cell function<br>⊕ May protect against some cancers<br>⊕ Reduces blood cholesterol levels, blood pressure and likelihood of blood clots, lowering the risk of heart disease and strokes<br>⊕ Helps rheumatoid arthritis due to anti-inflammatory properties<br>⊕ Improves circulation and skin disorders such as psoriasis and dermatitis | ❶ Eat fresh tuna, mackerel, salmon, herrings, anchovies and sardines twice a week |
| **Olive Oil** | ➲ VITAMIN E<br>➲ MONOUNSATURATED FAT | ⊕ Antioxidant properties help to protect against heart disease, effectively reducing blood cholesterol levels<br>⊕ Reduces the risk of certain cancers<br>⊕ Eases arthritis<br>⊕ May help liver and gallbladder problems<br>⊕ Improves digestion | ❶ Buy the best quality olive oil you can afford |
| **Onion** | ➲ QUERCETIN (ANTIOXIDANT)<br>➲ VITAMINS A & C<br>➲ MANGANESE<br>➲ IRON<br>➲ PHOSPHORUS | ⊕ Reduces the risk of heart disease and strokes, thinning the blood and reducing harmful cholesterol levels<br>⊕ Protects against some cancers, particularly stomach<br>⊕ Antibacterial and antiviral, helping to fight colds, relieve bronchial congestion, asthma and hayfever<br>⊕ Effective against arthritis, gout and rheumatism | ❶ Healing properties are more prevalent when raw |

| FOOD | NUTRIENTS | HELPS & HEALS | TIPS |
|---|---|---|---|
| **Orange** | ➲ Vitamin C<br>➲ Beta carotene<br>➲ Bioflavonoids | ⊕ High vitamin C content helps to protect against many forms of cancer, particularly stomach and oesophagus<br>⊕ Protects against heart attacks and strokes, reducing blood cholesterol levels<br>⊕ Boosts immune system and fights colds and flu | ❶ Best eaten soon after peeling, since oranges lose their vitamin C content as soon as they are cut |
| **Parsley** | ➲ Iron<br>➲ Vitamins A & C<br>➲ Calcium<br>➲ Manganese<br>➲ Potassium | ⊕ Diuretic and blood purifier<br>⊕ Helps eliminate uric acid, benefiting sufferers of gout and rheumatism<br>⊕ Counters anaemia | ❶ A useful source of calcium for people who don't eat dairy products |
| **Pea** | ➲ Vitamin C<br>➲ Thiamin (B1)<br>➲ Fibre<br>➲ Folate<br>➲ Phosphorus & iron | ⊕ Helps to reduce blood cholesterol levels, reducing the risk of heart disease<br>⊕ Fibre helps to steady blood sugar levels | ❶ Fresh peas have to be extremely fresh to be as nutritious as frozen |
| **Pepper (sweet)** | ➲ Vitamins C & E<br>➲ Beta carotene<br>➲ Iron<br>➲ Potassium<br>➲ Bioflavonoids | ⊕ High antioxidant properties, known to reduce the risk of heart disease, strokes, cataracts and some forms of cancer<br>⊕ Good for skin and bones | ❶ Best avoided by those with joint problems as peppers are members of the deadly nightshade family<br>❶ Red and orange peppers contain more vitamin C than green |
| **Pineapple** | • Vitamins A, C & E<br>• Potassium<br>• Calcium<br>• Phosphorus | ⊕ Contains the enzyme bromelain which has anti-inflammatory and antibacterial properties<br>⊕ Relieves arthritis<br>⊕ Aids digestion and improves circulation<br>⊕ May help angina | ❶ Fresh pineapple is better for you than canned |

| FOOD | NUTRIENTS | HELPS & HEALS | TIPS |
|---|---|---|---|
| **Pulses** | ⮕ B VITAMINS<br>⮕ IRON<br>⮕ FOLATE<br>⮕ POTASSIUM<br>⮕ FIBRE | ⊕ Lowers blood cholesterol levels by about 20 per cent if eaten regularly, reducing the risk of heart disease and strokes<br>⊕ Helps to control blood sugar levels, so valuable for diabetics<br>⊕ Reduces blood pressure<br>⊕ Helps anaemia | ❶ Excellent source of low-fat protein for vegetarians |
| **Rice (brown)** | ⮕ B VITAMINS<br>⮕ IRON<br>⮕ FIBRE<br>⮕ POTASSIUM<br>⮕ MAGNESIUM | ⊕ Helps to control blood sugar levels, making it useful for diabetics<br>⊕ May help with psoriasis<br>⊕ Aids digestive disorders and calms the nervous system<br>⊕ Reduces the risk of bowel and colon cancer and also kidney stones | ❶ Brown rice contains more nutrients than refined white |
| **Seaweed** | ⮕ VITAMIN B12<br>⮕ IODINE<br>⮕ CALCIUM<br>⮕ IRON<br>⮕ MAGNESIUM<br>⮕ ZINC | ⊕ Improves condition of hair<br>⊕ Benefits the nervous system, helping to reduce stress<br>⊕ Boosts immune system and aids metabolism<br>⊕ Iodine helps thyroid function and prevents goitre<br>⊕ Helps to strengthen bones | ❶ Dried seaweed is now available in many supermarkets |
| **Seeds** | ⮕ VITAMIN E<br>⮕ OMEGA-6 FATTY ACIDS<br>⮕ IRON<br>⮕ ZINC<br>⮕ FIBRE | ⊕ Vitamin E (especially high in sunflower seeds) protects cells from oxidation, improves circulation and normal blood clotting<br>⊕ Reduces risk of heart disease and strokes by lowering blood cholesterol levels<br>⊕ Pumpkin seeds promote good prostate health<br>⊕ Reduces risk of some cancers<br>⊕ Supports the immune system and has restorative qualities | ❶ Try to eat a variety of seeds, including sunflower, pumpkin, sesame and linseeds |
| **Shellfish** | ⮕ VITAMIN B12<br>⮕ SELENIUM<br>⮕ IODINE & ZINC<br>⮕ CALCIUM<br>⮕ IRON<br>⮕ OMEGA-3 FATTY ACIDS | ⊕ Maintains the nervous system and regulates metabolism<br>⊕ Helps to reduce the risk of some cancers and protects against heart disease and circulation problems<br>⊕ Strengthens the immune system<br>⊕ Known as an aphrodisiac<br>⊕ Anti-inflammatory benefits | ❶ Recent research dismisses any link between shellfish and high cholesterol. It may, in fact, reduce cholesterol levels |

| FOOD | NUTRIENTS | HELPS & HEALS | TIPS |
|------|-----------|---------------|------|
| **Soya Bean** | ⮕ COMPLETE PROTEIN<br>⮕ B VITAMINS<br>⮕ IRON<br>⮕ FOLATE & CALCIUM<br>⮕ POTASSIUM<br>⮕ FIBRE | ⊕ Contain phytoestrogens, known to protect against cancer of the breast, prostate and colon. Helps to balance hormone levels<br>⊕ Reduces the risk of osteoporosis<br>⊕ Reduces blood cholesterol levels and blood pressure<br>⊕ Eases constipation and helps fight bowel disease<br>⊕ Regulates blood sugar levels | ❶ Tofu, tempeh and miso are all soya bean products |
| **Spinach** | ⮕ BETA CAROTENE<br>⮕ VITAMIN C<br>⮕ IRON<br>⮕ CALCIUM & FOLATE<br>⮕ POTASSIUM<br>⮕ FIBRE | ⊕ Green leafy vegetables help to reduce the risk of cancer of the lung, stomach, prostate, bladder and skin<br>⊕ Rich in antioxidants, reducing the risk of heart disease, cataracts and strokes<br>⊕ Helps to regulate high blood pressure<br>⊕ Fights fatigue and mental strain | ❶ Eating spinach with a vitamin C-rich food will help your body absorb its iron content |
| **Sweet Potato** | ⮕ BETA CAROTENE<br>⮕ VITAMINS C & E<br>⮕ POTASSIUM<br>⮕ FIBRE<br>⮕ IRON | ⊕ Good for the heart<br>⊕ Reduces the risk of some cancers<br>⊕ Improves condition of the skin<br>⊕ Helps to regulate high blood pressure<br>⊕ Cleanses and detoxifies the system, boosting circulation<br>⊕ Beneficial levels of iron help combat anaemia | ❶ The orange-fleshed sweet potato has a higher nutritional content than the cream-fleshed variety |
| **Tomato** | ⮕ VITAMINS C & E<br>⮕ BETA CAROTENE<br>⮕ MAGNESIUM<br>⮕ POTASSIUM<br>⮕ CALCIUM | ⊕ Contains the bioflavonoid lycopene, said to prevent some forms of cancer, particularly prostate<br>⊕ Antioxidant properties reduce the risk of heart disease, strokes and cataracts | ❶ Cooking enhances some of the health-giving qualities of tomatoes, particularly the effectiveness of lycopene<br>❶ Can trigger migraine, eczema and mouth ulcers |
| **Watercress** | ⮕ BETA CAROTENE<br>⮕ VITAMIN C & E<br>⮕ FOLATE<br>⮕ IRON<br>⮕ POTASSIUM | ⊕ Part of the cancer-fighting cruciferous family (also includes broccoli, cabbage, sprouts and cauliflower). Effective against cancers of the colon, rectum and bladder<br>⊕ Rich in antioxidants, helping to protect against heart disease and strokes<br>⊕ Natural antibiotic, boosting the immune system and helping relieve stomach and respiratory problems<br>⊕ Improves skin problems, including acne<br>⊕ Purifies the system and stimulates circulation | ❶ At its most nutritious during the summer months |

| FOOD | NUTRIENTS | HELPS & HEALS | TIPS |
|------|-----------|---------------|------|
| **Wheat** | ➲ B vitamins & E<br>➲ Iron<br>➲ Zinc<br>➲ Fibre<br>➲ Selenium | ⊕ Fibre helps protect against colon and bowel cancer, varicose veins, haemorrhoids and obesity<br>⊕ Phytoestrogens in wholegrains may reduce risk of breast cancer and alleviate menopausal symptoms<br>⊕ Eases constipation<br>⊕ Wheatgrass is a powerful detoxifier and cleanser | ❶ Wheat is an allergen and should be avoided by those with coeliac disease |
| **Yogurt** | ➲ Calcium<br>➲ B vitamins<br>➲ Phosphorus | ⊕ The 'good' bacteria in live yogurt suppresses harmful bacteria in the gut, so aiding digestion and relieving gastrointestinal problems<br>⊕ Restores intestinal flora if consumed after a course of antibiotics<br>⊕ Can protect against thrush<br>⊕ May reduce the risk of colon cancer | ❶ Choose natural live bio yogurt |

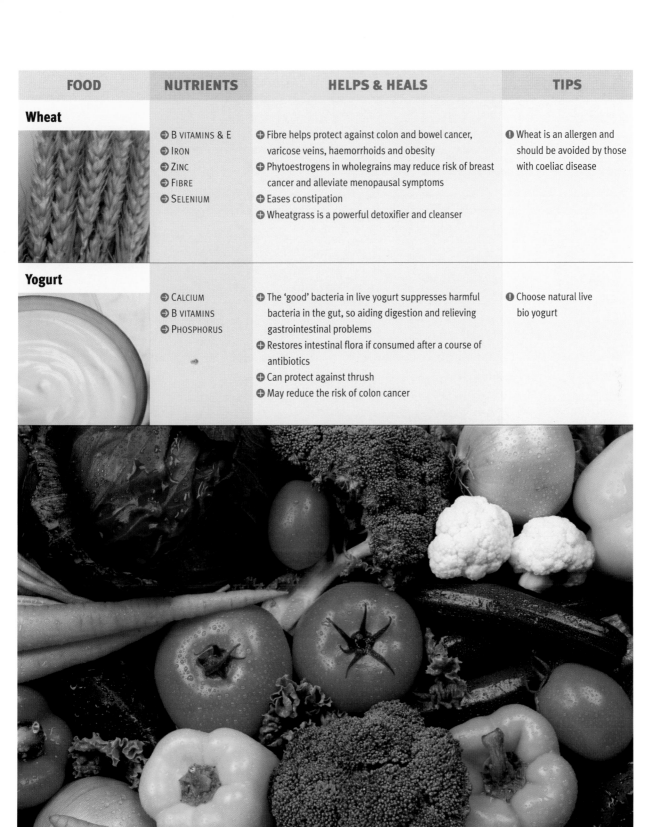

# further information

## WEBSITES

Alcohol Concern
www.alcoholconcern.org.uk

Arthritic Association
www.arthriticassociation.org.uk

British Allergy Foundation
www.allergyfoundation.com

British Association of Dermatologists
www.skinhealth.co.uk

British Dietetic Association
www.bda.uk.com

British Dental Association
www.bda.org

British Heart Foundation
www.bhf.org.uk

British Nutrition Foundation
www.nutrition.org.uk

Cancer Research Campaign
www.crc.org.uk

Department of Health
www.doh.gov.uk

Diabetes UK
www.diabetes.org.uk

Eating Disorders Association
www.edauka.com

Healthy Forum
www.thehealthyforum.com

Imperial Cancer Research Fund
www.icnet.uk

National Association for Colitis and Crohn's Disease
www.nacc.org.uk

National Asthma Campaign
www.asthma.org.uk

# ADDRESSES

**Alcohol Concern**
Waterbridge House
32–36 Loman Street
London SW1 OEE
Tel: 020 7928 7377

**Arthritic Association**
First Floor Suite
2 Hyde Gardens
Eastbourne
East Sussex BN21 4PN
Tel: 01323 416550

**British Allergy Foundation**
Deepdene House
30 Bellegrove Road
Welling
Kent DA16 3PY
Tel: 020 8303 8583

**British Dietetic Association**
5th Floor
Elizabeth House
22 Suffolk Street
Queensway
Birmingham
Tel: 0121 6164900

**British Heart Foundation**
14 Fitzhardinge Street
London W1H 4DH
020 7935 0185

**British Nutrition Foundation**
High Holborn House
52–54 High Holborn
London WC1V 6RQ
Tel: 020 7404 6504

**Cancer Research Campaign**
10 Cambridge Terrace
London NW1 4JL
Tel: 020 7224 1333

**Department of Health**
Richmond House
79 Whitehall
London SW1A 2NL
Tel: 020 7210 3000

**Diabetes UK**
10 Queen Anne Street
London W1M 0BD
Tel: 020 7636 6112

**Eating Disorders Association**
First Floor
Wensum House
103 Prince of Wales Road
Norwich NR1 1DW
Tel: 01603 621 414

**Imperial Cancer Research Fund**
44 Lincoln's Inn Fields
London WC2A 3PX
Tel: 020 7242 0200

**National Association for Colitis
and Crohn's Disease**
4 Beaumont House
Sutton Road
St Albans
Herts AL1 5HH
Tel: 01727 830038

**National Asthma Campaign**
Providence House
Providence Place
London N1 0NT
Tel: 020 7226 2260

# index

# acknowledgements

## Picture credits

CORBIS:
p.6 Michael Keller; p.15 Stephen Welstead;
Tom & Dee Ann McCarthy; p.26 Jutta Klee;
p.28 Lou Chardonnay; p.30 Lou Chardonnay;
p.32 David Raymer; p.34 Steve Thornton

## Author acknowledgements

I would like to thank Cathy Herbert for her meticulous editing. My gratitude also goes to Jason Hook at Bridgewater Books for commissioning me to write this book. Thanks, too, to the home economist Richard Green and photographer Ian Parsons.